Wise Growth Strategies in Leading Family Businesses

Wise Growth Strategies in Leading Family Businesses

Joachim Schwass

© Joachim Schwass 2005

All rights reserved. No reproduction, copy or transmission of this publication may be made without written permission.

No paragraph of this publication may be reproduced, copied or transmitted save with written permission or in accordance with the provisions of the Copyright, Designs and Patents Act 1988, or under the terms of any licence permitting limited copying issued by the Copyright Licensing Agency, 90 Tottenham Court Road, London W1T 4LP.

Any person who does any unauthorised act in relation to this publication may be liable to criminal prosecution and civil claims for damages.

The author has asserted his right to be identified as the author of this work in accordance with the Copyright, Designs and Patents Act 1988.

First published 2005 by
PALGRAVE MACMILLAN
Houndmills, Basingstoke, Hampshire RG21 6XS and
175 Fifth Avenue, New York, N.Y. 10010
Companies and representatives throughout the world

PALGRAVE MACMILLAN is the global academic imprint of the Palgrave Macmillan division of St Martin's Press LLC and of Palgrave Macmillan Ltd.
Macmillan® is a registered trademark in the United States, United Kingdom and other countries. Palgrave is a registered trademark in the European Union and other countries.

ISBN-13: 978–1–4039–9416–5 hardback
ISBN-10: 1–4039–9416–1 hardback

This book is printed on paper suitable for recycling and made from fully managed and sustained forest sources.

A catalogue record for this book is available from the British Library.

Library of Congress Cataloging-in-Publication Data
Schwass, Joachim, 1950–
  Wise growth strategies in leading family businesses / by Joachim Schwass.
    p. cm.
  Includes bibliographical references and index.
  ISBN 1–4039–9416–1 (cloth)
   1. Family-owned business enterprises—Growth. 2. Family-owned business enterprises—Case studies. I. Title.

HD62.25.S37 2005
338.7—dc22

2005047525

10 9 8 7 6 5 4 3 2 1
14 13 12 11 10 09 08 07 06 05

Printed and bound in Great Britain by
Antony Rowe Ltd, Chippenham and Eastbourne

For
Nina, Alex, Fred and Max

Contents

List of tables and figures	ix
Foreword	x
An interview with Peter Lorange, President, IMD	
A unique award	xvi
Thierry Lombard, Lombard Odier Darier Hentsch	
Preface	xviii
Acknowledgements	xxi
Introduction	**1**
Insights gained from the world's leading family businesses	2
1 Summaries of award-winning family businesses	**6**
The LEGO Group	6
Hermès	9
Corporacion Puig	11
The Henkel Group	13
The Zegna Group	16
The Murugappa Group	18
Samuel C. Johnson Family Enterprises	21
The Bonnier Group	23
The Barilla Group	26
2 Threats to multigenerational survival of family businesses	**29**
The three family business archetypes	30
Is the family a threat to survival?	32
The most important threat to survival: general transitions	35
What does this mean for the next-generation leader in a family business?	36
The risk of failure is very real	38
What are the real challenges for next-generation leaders?	39

3 Understanding the family business leadership challenges	**42**
What do they want?	44
What do these lists tell us?	45
The change initiative	46
Transition is evolution – not revolution	47
The leadership phases matrix	56
4 The "wise growth" strategy	**60**
Wise growth: growing as an individual	62
Wise growth: growing the role in the business	75
Wise growth: growing the business	89
5 Conclusion	**97**
Appendix A: Family business – an important, developing field of research	99
Appendix B: Distinguished Family Business Award	101
Distinguished Family Business Award Winners – 1996–2004	102
Appendix C: The articles on the nine award-winning family businesses	103
The LEGO Group	103
Hermès	108
Corporacion Puig	112
The Henkel Group	118
The Zegna Group	124
The Murugappa Group	132
Samuel C. Johnson Family Enterprises	140
The Bonnier Group	146
The Barilla Group	156
References	162
Index	162

List of Tables and Figures

Tables

2.1	Family: opportunity and threat for the business	34
3.1	The successor's challenges by interest level in the "do" phase	52
3.2	The successor's challenges by interest level in the "lead to do" phase	54
3.3	The successor's challenges by interest level in the "let do" phase	56
3.4	The leadership phases matrix	56
3.5	Stakeholder's interest by objective	58
4.1	Generational growth strategies: Henkel	91
4.2	Generational growth strategies: Bonnier	91
4.3	Generational growth strategies: Zegna	91
4.4	Zegna: generational business growth strategies	92
A.1	Compass Management: a process of changing attitudes and behaviours	106
A.2	Barilla Group revenues and EBITDA per subsidiary in 2003	160

Figures

3.1	Generational leadership cycle	48
4.1	Wise growth strategy	62

Foreword

An interview with Peter Lorange, President, IMD

Joachim Schwass [JS]: Why does IMD support a special award for family businesses?

Peter Lorange [PL]: The main reason is that family business is a very important part of the value creation equation, a very important part of growth in society by generating jobs and new wealth. Family businesses also bring new dynamics to society. Our research here at IMD shows that family-owned firms often outperform widely held, publicly owned firms. We believe that family business is a vital area – hence the Distinguished Family Business Award. The problem with family businesses is that they often get very little feedback, unlike publicly traded companies that receive feedback from the marketplace through analysts' write-ups. In a public corporation, you celebrate when your stock is doing well or when you have an offering of funds, but there are no such celebrations when you have a family business. In addition, the internal fabric of a family business works in such a way that the feedback mechanism, on performance for example, may be a bit twisted. Brilliant up-and-coming family business board or management team members will often be told that they were born with a silver spoon in their mouth, and whatever strengths they have tend to be discounted because they are perceived to have been born into the job. So a successor may get a kind of orphan or "anti" feedback reality whatever he or she does, and this is similar to what happens with the recognition of family business from the outside. Therefore it is important that, through the award, we show the world the best practices of family business. It is very much part of our research agenda and of our institutional value set and commitment.

JS: What do you perceive to be the important success factors of family businesses?

PL: I think that there are several success factors. The one that is most commonly focused on in the research is succession and its related issues – making sure that succession takes place in such a way that the interests of the family, the firm and the individuals evolve in as harmonious a way as possible. Disharmony, by implication, could mean that energy might be wasted and that the firm's performance might decline and the wealth of the family would be sub-optimized. There are two other important factors, which both have to do with the growth of the business itself. One could argue that perhaps they are not directly linked to family business, but they are. The first is that there are often silos in organizations – in family businesses there may be particularly nasty silo tendencies. One son says that he wants to run a particular side of the business by himself, and that he needs to be sheltered from the rest of the family because his sisters and brothers, cousins, uncles and aunts can be difficult, and he needs to carve out a little kingdom for himself. If there are a number of instances like this, then there are silos. Furthermore, this can also create silos among the professional members of the management team because they look to these family members. I have seen a lot of this in family businesses, and it is the antithesis of growth. It is harder to grow if members of the family hold all the important positions. The culture is "Don't touch my domain, this is my turf". Obviously, this exists in all organizations, but in family businesses the problems are compounded. So the second success factor would be that family businesses should try to avoid silos.

A third success factor has to do with the role of the internal entrepreneur in the family business. Professor Chakravarthy and I have carried out research that strongly points to the role of internal entrepreneurs in larger companies. When it comes to pushing growth, they are people who stick their necks out to get something done. Often, they are sponsored by a senior executive who shelters them against too many vicious attacks from the business bureaucracy.

The problem in family businesses is that this process can often go astray. The family members want to be in command. They want to be involved in any entrepreneurial activity that directly involves their "purse", since it is their money and their firm. They want to run these entrepreneurial activities. I have experienced this myself with my own shipping company, which I own 100 per cent. I want to make these entrepreneurial investment decisions myself. I do not want my managing director to do it – it's my money. And that is precisely the problem. You may end up with a less powerful entrepreneurial drive in many family firms because there is very little incentive for an individual to try to be an internal entrepreneur. He or she knows that this goes against the values of the family firm.

JS: Does this potentially put family businesses at a competitive disadvantage?

PL: I think so, because all three points I'm making can lead to failure. I certainly see a lot of succession planning done very poorly. It is easier for a public firm to do succession planning.

JS: Why is this?

PL: It is easier because the board defines the overall governance structure. People are elected to the board; ownership and governance are not so entangled. In a family firm, the leaders or board members are often the owners, and you can't kick them out, as it so often becomes a family consideration. This is a potential disadvantage for the family, for the governance process and for the succession process. A second disadvantage can be the above-mentioned silo issue, and the third disadvantage is the lack of entrepreneurs. These are areas where family firms are at a disadvantage. When it comes to long-term thinking, willingness to invest with a long-term payoff, willingness to stick it out, the ability to be robust without any dissident stakeholders, these are distinct pluses for family firms.

JS: What can public corporations learn from family businesses?

PL: I think the most phenomenal issue is the dilemma of long-term versus short-term objectives and achieving a happy balance between the two. Public firms can learn a lot. There is no doubt that publicly traded firms are very short-term oriented. Growth and top line are all important. To create true value, also for stockholders in publicly traded firms, you need to consistently grow both the top and the bottom line as both have short- and long-term points of view. It is a more natural dilemma to deal with in family-owned firms, where there is typically more of a long-term philosophy combined with a healthy short-term focus. Maybe another issue for family members in a family business is that they are there to stay while in publicly traded companies there often is a lot of politics. There is politicking in family businesses, too, but perhaps the fact that you can't remove people so easily from many family firms makes it imperative to learn how to deal effectively with conflicts. I was, for instance, very impressed by the Michelin company, which has three managing directors with a ten-year age difference. One is around 70, another is around 60 and the third around 50. One of the three tends to be a member of the Michelin family, but with this trio working together, you get some tremendous family continuity combined with outside views.

JS: In many ways, the strength of the family business lies in being able to refer back to some continuity, rather than going through a repetition of quantum leaps and innovation bounds when a new leader comes in. The challenge here is how does the next generation leader innovate, linking tradition with innovation?

PL: Maybe the new generation could be internal entrepreneurs and work with the older guard to inspire business rather than being kept away or dumped on.

JS: Family businesses are well known for their strong value system. How does that fit into today's environment?

PL: I think you can find strong values in many companies today, whether they are family businesses or not. Undoubtedly, there have been some very dramatic public corporation shortcomings: Enron, Parmalat and Skandia to mention just a few. But I think that, fundamentally, it is hard to say that family firms necessarily have stronger values than publicly traded firms. I think you can find very good publicly traded firms with strong values.

JS: But are family businesses in a better position to leverage or express the values in a more believable way?

PL: There is no hard and fast rule. You can have very corrupt family firms, but you can also have corrupt publicly traded firms. It can go both ways.

JS: You are the head of a great learning organization and education institute, and you have seen many managers who are not part of a family business benefiting from learning opportunities and developing themselves. In your eyes, could family business leaders benefit from a learning experience at IMD?

PL: It depends. I think the issue of learning today has a lot to do with the global meeting place. In a sense, if you accept that a lot of dilemmas facing you, as a manager today, can be best understood if you have a variety of viewpoints from different parts of the world. For example, a Brazilian might see issues differently from a Japanese, a Canadian differently from a South African, an Australian differently from a Swiss. I think that the premise is to accept diversity. Now, the bad news for some family firms is that they are often more deeply – individually and emotionally – connected to their birthplace than larger public corporations. If you take many of the German Mittelstand companies, their roots are German, the families are German, and they are perhaps less inclined to come to this kind of global meeting and thinking place. I've seen several family company members say, "It's not for me." Most of my family comes from Norway, but you cannot run the family company as if we have all the answers to shipping in Norway – it would be a disaster.

Family businesses need to be more open and transparent. They need to develop a curiosity for other businesses and learn what public corporations and other family businesses from other parts of the world are doing better. Here at IMD, we believe in the learning benefits created by a dynamic and eclectic global melting pot.

A unique award

Thierry Lombard, Lombard Odier Darier Hentsch

The English language has different words to express the idea of a gift honouring a special merit. For Nobel, Pulitzer and Ansari, it is called a prize. For Lombard Odier Darier Hentsch (LODH), it is called an award. Is there a difference?

Etymologically, the word "prize", as shown by its proximity to the word "price", insists on the value that the prize is meant to acknowledge. To give someone a prize is to rank them on a scale, letting everyone know who is first and adding a value (the prize) to an estimated value (the price).

Giving an award is slightly different. The etymology of the word "award" has nothing to do with prizing or pricing. Coming from Old French, it originally meant "to decide, to examine, after careful observation and consideration". It places the emphasis on the examination rather than on the mark and attaches a value to the observation rather than the ranking.

This is exactly the philosophy of the IMD-LODH Family Business Award. It is far away from any scales of triple A, double Y or a simple Moody's ranking. The winners may be 200 or 40 years old, may be Spanish, French or Danish; they may produce toys, perfumes, food or clothes.

The experts attributing the IMD-LODH Family Business Award do not merely count up or cast a detached glance at some lengthy columns of figures; they examine the financial, strategic and ethical aspects of the business with "careful consideration" that reveals who the people are running the business, where they go, how and on which values they grow. It is not pricing, but rather an understanding of a whole corporate identity including a family and business personality and a set of best practices; therefore, it is an award and not a prize.

This book's method is perfectly aligned with the guiding principles of the IMD-LODH Family Business Award. Rather than telling nine stories of successful, award-winning family businesses, it tries to look further, with "careful observation", at what makes these businesses so successful and wise. As the IMD-LODH Family Business Award has made these businesses "exemplary", Joachim Schwass takes on the challenge, literally, of drawing real and useful models for every family business from these examples. In other words, there have so far been nine businesses worthy of an award, so isn't the award now worthy of a book?

For over 200 years and through seven generations, Lombard Odier Darier Hentsch has had the privilege of listening to, advising and accompanying entrepreneurs and families. This responsibility – as independent private bankers and partners in a position of trust – has allowed us to understand the main characteristics and special features of family businesses. We are therefore proud and delighted to have been associated for the past nine years with the awarding of a distinction that recognizes such long-term excellence and achievement in the service of family businesses worldwide.

Preface

My first exposure to family business was at home. Growing up in a family business adds something special – another component to your life. There are two ways of experiencing this component: either as a burden or as something enriching.

It can be a burden in the sense of limiting freedom and choices. There is a sense of predetermination with the business taking priority over everything else. The implicit and explicit expectation is that the family and the next generation need to look after the business and need to serve in the business. After all, isn't it the business that provides the financial resources to the family? Doesn't this justify the expectation that the next generation should also serve in the business?

But there is another view: a family business can be enriching to the family and its individual members. Yes, enriching financially but, more importantly, in intangible ways that provide opportunities for personal growth. Opportunities which are based on learning how businesses function, understanding how real value is created in a market, and discovering why people believe in this business, both as employees and as outside stakeholders. Family business histories and legends are also enriching as they provide a historical context to the members. Members grow up steeped in the history of how the business was started – why and how did the originator actually become an entrepreneur, as well as understanding how the business evolved throughout the generations. This family history could contribute to both the "burden" and "enrichment" scales.

The difference between these two mindsets has enormous implications, mostly for the individual leader. What role do passion and the motivational power of free choice play? If you decide, as an individual, what you want to do and then fully immerse yourself into it, simply because it is your own choice, then you will probably fall into the "enrichment" mindset. If, on the other hand, you decide to take a role in the family business out of obligation, rather than genuine interest, then you are more likely to fall into the "burden" mindset.

When I entered the professional and academic world of family business, I was struck by the documentation that showed a high failure rate in family businesses, particularly around generational transitions. These failures were seen as business failures, but a deeper post-mortem analysis invariably pointed to the original failure occurring at the family level. Over the years of encountering families in businesses from around the world, my observation is that there are infinitely more unhappy family members than happy ones. Is this a necessary byproduct of family businesses evolving over multiple generations, or the seed for failure in the future?

My search for a reply began over nine years ago. We set out to identify leading family businesses from around the world that were multigenerational and successful: not just surviving family businesses, but the best ones. The criteria for best were stringent and essentially built on the most effective, long-term and value-added linkages between the families that owned the businesses and the businesses themselves. We looked for family businesses which could provide guidelines for reducing wasted resources – both financial and, more importantly, human. We also searched for family businesses which could provide an inspiration in finding a constructive, collectively and individually meaningful reply to the question that each generation must ask itself first and foremost: "Why continue the family business?"

I believe this question to be of fundamental importance for the continuity of a family business. In my personal experience, from today's perspective, I very much regret that this question was not formally addressed in our own family business. I believe this led to inefficiencies which could have been avoided. In my professional experience, observing and researching family businesses from around the world, only a small minority consider the true and real issues that this question addresses. I believe that it is this minority that manages to achieve the best equilibrium in addressing the needs of all four family business constituents: family, ownership, management and the individual. Family businesses that successfully span many generations understand that the key ingredient for sustainability is to "start at the beginning", namely addressing the needs of the individuals first. If it is so simple, why don't more family businesses do this? The surprising insight from my nine years of research is that the successful family businesses handle this issue in a two-step approach.

Firstly, the next generation of family members is generally deeply immersed in the family and business culture; often in surprisingly strong and locked-in ways. But, at a certain point in time, this lock-in approach is lifted and gives way to a culture of individual freedom which often reflects the characteristics found in first generation founders and entrepreneurs. It is this development process which has led to outstanding success for the award-winning family businesses in this book. The point at which a new generation of leaders switches from the "locked-in" culture to the "entrepreneurial" culture is of particular interest. In some cases, it is chance or fate that triggered the change; in other cases, it is part of a master plan. Grasping the mechanics of this process and understanding the potential benefits of proactive planning is at the heart of this book.

I hope that the insights I have gained from the last nine years of research can help two audiences: firstly, those family businesses that are concerned with a long-term future and, secondly, all of the individual family members – both those that have an active role in the family business and those with more passive roles – that are helping the family move toward that future.

Joachim Schwass

Acknowledgements

Many people deserve thanks for having supported – knowingly and unknowingly – the creation of this book:

Peter Lorange, President of IMD, both by supporting the IMD-LODH Distinguished Family Business Award and the encouragement to write – and complete – this book;
Thierry Lombard, Senior Partner of LODH, by supporting the Award and his inspiring deep commitment to researching family businesses;
John L. Ward, my "partner" at IMD, by his never-ending search for more and better family business knowledge, and the hint that it is better to be wise than smart (thanks, John!);
Alden (Alli) G. Lank, who inspired me and took the risk of bringing a rookie into the academic world;
Richard Owens, who started the connection from down under (thanks, mate!);
Fred Neubauer, whose gentle discipline kept me going;
Tom Bata and Jonathan Pellegrin, who both launched the first award and successfully got it off the ground;
Gordon Adler, for his never-ending and deeply appreciated support in getting me unstuck numerous times;
Ivan Moss, who knows more about family business than he thinks and who made me work harder on finding a better logic;
Nancy Lane, who double-checked the content fault lines;
Beverley Lennox, whose patience and sense of details in correcting the script is truly admirable;
Megan Price, who – always smiling – took on the word-processing challenge; Colleen Lief, for her efficient research support;
Susanne Hanson, whose persistent commitment to helping family businesses through better knowledge is inspiring.

Two final thanks:

Firstly to all of the nine award-winning family businesses who have so generously shared their deepest knowledge and their unique experiences; lastly, to all members of my family – each one has somehow had a meaningful impact on this book.

My heartfelt thanks go to all.

Joachim Schwass

The author and publisher acnowledges permission to reproduce tables from Schwass (2005) published by John Wiley & Sons Ltd.

Introduction

As I said in the Preface, I wrote this book with family businesses in mind. I would like to address all members – the active leaders, those in the background with more supporting roles and those who aspire to have active leadership roles when their generation is ready. I hope to share some of the insights that I have gained through my research about what makes a family business more likely to succeed and how to put those learnings into practice in your family business.

This book had its beginnings in 1996 when IMD, celebrating its 50th anniversary as a business school, launched the annual Distinguished Family Business Award. We had two objectives: the first was to highlight family businesses' broad macroeconomic importance; the second was to identify successful family businesses and to learn what it is they do better than others. In order to identify the award winners, we established a stringent nomination and selection process, which is described in Appendix B. Candidates have to meet the following seven criteria in order to qualify for the Distinguished Family Business Award:

1. The family business has survived at least three generations
2. It has achieved a solid, long-term record of financial performance and stability
3. It produces products which are market leaders and are respected in their industry
4. It has established and maintained an effective governance system
5. It is an international business
6. It has effectively linked tradition and innovation.
7. It has demonstrated good corporate citizenship by making social contributions to the communities within which it operates.

Insights gained from the world's leading family businesses

After researching the world's leading family businesses for nine years, I have gained some important insights and learned a number of valuable lessons.

Firstly, and perhaps not surprisingly, there is no model for the perfect family business: not a single family business has done everything right for all of its stakeholders all of the time. Secondly, some important commonalities started to emerge. The most obvious common factor was the ability, over multiple generations, to adapt to both external and internal changes. External changes originate from the market (for example, controlled pricing after World War II, and opening up markets) and internal changes originate from the family and the business (for example, the unexpected death of a family business leader). The award-winning family businesses were able to build meaningfully on their history and traditions and to make necessary decisions that successfully led the family business toward their future: the next generation's leaders.

The insight that I took away from this research was that this adaptability over multiple generations followed a very clear logic. This logic, to the outside, is not always easily visible or understandable. In fact, some strategic adaptation may appear to be revolutionary and counterintuitive as seen from the outside. But these families applied their own benchmarks and a logic that, when seen from the inside, is evolutionary rather than revolutionary.

The families' logic manifested itself most obviously in both a business growth strategy that successfully adapted to changing markets, and the families' ability to provide highly effective leadership that drove and executed this strategy.

Lesson 1 from the award-winning family businesses is a **business growth strategy** which draws on the inherent strengths and advantages family businesses have over widely owned (by widely owned or widely held, I mean a company with shares that are not concentrated in one person's or one family's hands) public corporations.

I next focused on who led these family businesses: who developed and implemented these successful business growth strategies? The award-winning family businesses all had produced successful leaders in each generation. Was this due to luck or planning? Certainly luck – and fate – had a certain influence. But it became clear, through my research, that leadership was made possible by the presence of a forward-oriented growth mentality that was deeply anchored in the mind of the family.

Lesson 2 from the award-winning family businesses is a **growth mindset**.

This insight became obvious when I analysed reasons why families occasionally prune their tree. Over time, some of the award-winning families actively eliminated certain members or branches who did not share their growth mindset. In some cases, these separations were painful for the family; in other cases, they were the result of a positive, spirited process. But the underlying motivation always appeared to be the unconditional, emotional attachment to a continuously growing business by some members of the family. This Darwinian selection process amongst family members, whereby only the strongest survive, led to the next important insight.

Lesson 3 from the award-winning family businesses is that the leaders submitted themselves to a **disciplined process of systematically growing as an individual and growing their role as leaders in the business**.

Those family members and branches who wanted to involve themselves in the business seemed, on one hand, driven by a forward-oriented growth mentality, and on the other hand, wise enough to see the complexities and inherent risks of owning a family business. The multiple interest levels – family, ownership, management and the individual – need to be acknowledged and each generation must, for themselves, create a well-balanced approach towards addressing the needs of these stakeholders. Therefore, the most essential and striking insights from the award-winning family businesses are:

- A coherent family vision based on growth
- The application of the growth concept beginning with the individual, then growing their role in the business and finally growing the business
- The wisdom of linking the needs of family, ownership, management and the individual together in a forward-driving growth momentum.

From these findings emerged the concept of "wise growth" which separates the award-winning family businesses from the others. Understanding what wise growth means and how it is executed is the objective of this book.

In practical terms, this book attempts to describe a systematic approach on how to develop successive generations of family business leaders. This approach covers the lifecycle of a leader over one generation of the family business, and proposes segmenting the lifecycle into three distinct phases which differ in characteristics and needs: "do", "lead to do" and finally "let do". It attempts to answer the question, "What meaningful process can a family member, who wants to become the business leader, follow in order to grow as an individual, grow their role in the business and, finally, grow the business?" It also attempts to identify the important risks and opportunities for stakeholders. The adopted perspective is from the family member aspiring to the leadership position. This book links the needs and the role of the individual to the needs of the family business which is described as a dynamic system.

The summaries in Chapter 1 introduce the nine family businesses upon which this research is based. At the end of each summary, the Best Practices section highlights key learnings that can be drawn from each case. Appendix A talks about the importance of family business research and Appendix B outlines the background, criteria and process for the Distinguished Family Business Award. An extended description of each award winner, based on articles published the year they received the award, can be found in Appendix C.

Chapters 2 and 3 are about the multiple challenges a family business and its potential and actual leaders face during overlapping leadership cycles with respect to each of the four interest levels found in the family business. Chapter 4 explores the three dimensions of the wise growth strategy path highlighting best practices from the award-winning family businesses. The book concludes with Chapter 5.

1
Summaries of Award-Winning Family Businesses

The Distinguished Family Business Award was initially created in 1996. Today it is awarded annually by IMD, in partnership with Lombard Odier Darier Hentsch. In addition to highlighting the important global economic contribution of family businesses, the award recognizes outstanding companies which have successfully blended family and business interests and identifies best practices which may be useful to other family businesses.

Following are brief summaries, based on the extended articles in Appendix C, of each of the award winners from 1996 to 2004. Both the summaries and the extended descriptions are based on the articles published in the years the awards were presented.

The LEGO Group

IMD Distinguished Family Business Award Winner 1996

Founded in 1932, the LEGO Group, with close to 9,000 employees worldwide, has consistently and successfully blended business and family interests.

The Great Depression of the 1930s, and the resulting financial catastrophes for many, nearly forced the founder, Ole Kirk Christiansen, and his fledgling carpentry business, into bankruptcy. Recognizing that people could not afford to build houses, he reinvented his business and began producing stepladders, ironing boards and wooden toys. Demand for the well-made toys (called LEGO – a combination of two Danish words, *"leg godt"*, meaning "play well") was strong, and new products were developed: the diversification that was created to save the company, in fact, became the company.

The family embraced a conservative attitude toward their balance sheet as a result of the financial problems caused by the Depression and some early management difficulties. They also felt a deep sense of responsibility to both their employees and their vendors and developed a reputation for honouring their financial obligations.

The founder's son, Godtfred Kirk Christiansen, began working in the company when he was only 12 years old. By the age of 18, he was designing new toy models. By age 24, he was his father's right-hand man, responsible for product development, sales and finance.

In 1949, the company introduced a primitive forerunner of what was to become the revolutionary plastic building bricks. These toy construction components were popular and represented an opportunity for significant growth. Then, in 1955, Godtfred perceived a gap in the children's toy market and launched the "LEGO System of Play" based on the building bricks. Considering that just six of the original eight studded bricks of the same colour can be put together in 102,981,500 different ways, the opportunities for creative play are virtually limitless. Every year, more than 100 new LEGO sets are added to the range, and around the same number are withdrawn. New elements, play themes and sets result from the hundreds of ideas that come out of six product development departments in Denmark, the US and Japan.

The globalization of the LEGO Group was nearly as systematic as the development and expansion of the product line. Beginning in neighbouring Norway, distribution was expanded throughout Europe. Subsequently, captive sales companies were established around the world. By the early 1970s, the LEGO Group had truly become a well-known global brand.

All of the LEGO Group's business activities have followed the guiding principle that it must be a good corporate citizen. The company has been recognized throughout the world for the positive contributions it has made to the development of young people. The LEGO Group funds an annual international prize of DKr. 1 million for individuals and/or groups which have promoted children's welfare, development or education.

From an early age, Godtfred Kirk Christiansen's son, Kjeld Kirk Kristiansen, developed a reputation as a skilled and imaginative LEGO builder. GKC looked to young Kjeld as a great source of product development ideas. When he finished school, Kjeld joined LEGO's German subsidiary, then obtained a commercial degree followed by an MBA.

After 15 years as President of the LEGO Group, a prolonged illness resulted in Kjeld taking an unplanned sabbatical. While Kjeld was convalescing, he realized that despite having sustained growth for more than four decades, LEGO markets were undergoing major changes due to globalization, information technology, the media revolution and related new lifestyles – so the approach of LEGO management would also have to change. On his return, Kjeld implemented a new management direction at the LEGO Group, aimed at changing the attitudes and behaviour of employees and laying the foundation for the long-term reinvention of the company.

Best practices – LEGO

- Early and active family involvement in the business in each generation
- Conservative financial management
- Linking tradition with innovation
- Strong corporate governance structure with non-family chairman
- Strong corporate citizenship.

Hermès

IMD Distinguished Family Business Award Winner 1997

Known as the world's ultimate luxury business, Hermès SA is a French manufacturer and marketer of upmarket luggage, apparel and accessories. From a nineteenth-century foundation in leather goods, the company has since diversified into silk goods, ready-to-wear clothing, watches and perfumes. Its ongoing dedication to family ownership and management, impeccable craftsmanship, and careful protection of the brand's mystique set Hermès apart from most other companies.

From the late 1980s until today, Hermès has been led by Jean-Louis Dumas, a fifth-generation descendant of the founder. He has been credited with building Hermès' worldwide retailing empire by directing an intense programme of geographic expansion. From 1986 to 1996, Hermès enjoyed average annual sales increases of 24 per cent. The company's explosive growth saw annual sales grow from US$50 million in 1978 to US$700 million by 1996, and its net profit grew even faster.

During the 1970s, the usual Hermès 5 per cent annual sales growth started to drop. To overcome the crisis, the company hired new clothing designers to revive the apparel line. In 1979, a youthful advertising campaign changed the Hermès label from the object of an older generation's nostalgia to the subject of young people's dreams.

The company took advantage of the resurgence in Hermès popularity, expanded its line of merchandise to 30,000 different items, quadrupled the number of Hermès-owned stores, from 15 in 1978 to 80 in 1996, and increased the total number of outlets to more than 225 worldwide.

Hermès' trademark – a horse-drawn carriage – harkens back to its original saddlery business. Founded in 1837 by Thierry Hermès, the firm gained a reputation as a producer of one-of-a-kind saddlery for

European noblemen and the first two generations focused on this business.

Faced with the ascent of the automobile and corresponding obsolescence of the carriage, third-generation Emile-Maurice Hermès diversified into travel and sports-related leather goods – luggage, wallets and handbags. Then in the 1920s, the company launched ready-to-wear clothing, leather-banded watches and leather gloves.

Robert Dumas, the fourth-generation owner, produced the first Hermès scarf in 1937. The famous Hermès "Kelly" bag, named in the 1950s after Princess Grace of Monaco, who was often photographed with the accessory, also helped burnish the brand image as an accoutrement for royalty and celebrities.

Jean-Louis Dumas was the fifth generation to take over the company's top position after the death of his father in 1978. He had first worked as a buyer for competitors before returning to the family firm in 1964.

Based on family consensus, Hermès made its first stock offering in June 1993. But the family retained over 80 per cent of the equity in the hands of 56 family members, six of whom kept a 5–10 per cent stake. Hermès has been able, despite being risk takers, to stick to the principle of self-financing. To avoid financial dependence on the banks, but still have the capital needed for new projects, Hermès traditionally reinvests approximately 15 per cent of its profits in the company.

Some observers consider Hermès scarves collectible works of art. Hermès' combination of quality materials and time-consuming hand craftsmanship is reflected in its high retail prices. In 2004, Hermès scarves were priced at US$295 each, a tie cost US$130, and a Kelly purse set cost over US$5,000.

Best practices – Hermès

- Strong family leadership over generations
- Each of the five generations added distinctive value to the business in an entrepreneurial way

- Effective linkage of tradition and innovation: "respect for new ideas"
- Deep generational commitment to quality
- Strong family culture
- Family values are transmitted through family education from generation to generation.

Corporacion Puig

IMD Distinguished Family Business Award Winner 1998

Long viewed as a prestigious company, the Barcelona-based Corporacion Puig is one of the few remaining family-owned perfume and fashion houses. Its various activities range from mass market products such as Aqua Brava and Quorum, to world-renowned brands such as Carolina Herrera, Paco Rabanne and Nina Ricci.

With growth rates of 15 per cent in the 1990s, Corporacion Puig regularly increased its market position, thanks to the development of prestigious branded products and remarkable geographic expansion.

Corporacion Puig was founded at the turn of the twentieth century when Antonio Puig established a small perfumery company. Later he caused something of a social outcry when he became the first Spanish lipstick manufacturer. According to family legend, in making lipstick, Antonio Puig encountered problems with the packaging – so he acquired his supplier's entire plant. This purchase launched a series of acquisitions that ultimately brought the company from a niche market player to a leading position in the fashion industry.

Antonio had four children who all took positions in the family business. In the mid-twentieth century, the company gradually came under the direction of Antonio Jr and Mariano. To give their product the market presence and fashionable, attractive image it needed, they were the first in the perfume industry to work with industrial designers and famous artists.

Once Antonio Jr and Mariano had the right product, they saw that Puig's research and development expenditures could not be recouped from the Spanish market. So, in the 1960s, they began an international expansion, setting up sales and distribution operations in the US, then Britain, Germany, Holland, Central America, South America, the Middle East and other regions. At the same time, the Puigs discovered that the Spanish product was not attractive enough for the US market. So they created a company in Paris, with its own product development, marketing and French personnel.

In the 1970s, Antonio Jr and Mariano realized that internal growth was insufficient to reach the critical mass needed to compete against the leading international groups. To stay independent they limited dividends to the family and purchased famous brand names with potential for expansion. International expansion also required reorganization of the management of the Puig group. The family appointed a non-family CEO, Javier Cano, who was an industrial engineer with 25 years' experience in various company positions.

To maintain family involvement as the family grew to four brothers in the second generation and to 14 cousins in the third generation, Corporacion Puig created a governing system made up of an assembly of shareholders, the holding (which supervised the various family companies), a family council and an advisory board with family and non-family members. Subsequently, a family handbook (code of principles, values and behaviour for family and employees) and a family protocol (an evolving set of rules for reconciling family and business interests) have been created by the family council.

In 1979, on his death bed, Antonio senior, the founder, left his children a testament that still guides the family, "Stay together. Your unity will be your strength." As in many family organizations, the Puigs consider their greatest challenge is to ensure the continuity of the business. Throughout the 1990s, they drew up an organizational and strategic plan to define their future objectives and guide the transition to the next generation.

In July 1998, the second generation – Antonio Jr and Mariano – officially retired from the operational business. The handover of control from the second to the third generation was staged as a formal event, with multiple stakeholders present. Executive power passed to a new executive committee of three family members and one non-family manager, Javier Cano. Mariano, of the second generation, became president of the board of directors. His brother, Antonio, became president of the shareholders' assembly.

Best practices – Puig

- Strong team family leadership of the business
- Strategic generational planning
- Multiple-level governance structures
- Code of conduct and rules for family members
- Strong family values
- Formal visioning and handover process from the second generation to the third.

The Henkel Group

IMD Distinguished Family Business Award Winner 1999

The Henkel Group, headquartered in Düsseldorf, Germany, is a large family-controlled business active in detergents, chemical products, adhesives and hygiene and surface technologies. The fourth generation today exercises an active ownership role.

Having seen that detergents could vastly facilitate household cleaning and washing, Fritz Henkel, the son of a schoolteacher, started a modest business selling bleaching soda in 1876. By 1899, he employed 79 workers and required a new location. His entrepreneurial ambition was clearly demonstrated by the size of the land he purchased for future development: 54,846 square metres.

In 1907, Fritz launched the first branded detergent product under the name Persil. The brand provided users with a guarantee of consistent product quality. Fritz also launched the first prepackaged detergent in a smaller household size. These innovations laid the groundwork for the future growth of the company. In 1908, the first conveyor belt packaging line for Persil products was introduced, and by 1911, employment had grown to 925.

In an unconventional approach for that period, Fritz split ownership of his business amongst his three children. His daughter, not active in the business, received 20 per cent. The sons, who had joined the business, were given 40 per cent each. The legacy of the founder to his children was that they must stay united as a family in the business.

In 1930, employment had surged to 5,000 workers with an annual production of over 110,000 tons, the vast majority being Persil washing powder. That year both Fritz and one of his sons died. Hugo, the surviving son, became leader of the company. In 1938, Hugo's oldest son, Jost, was appointed CEO, and Hugo became chairman of the supervisory board. Jost, the third generation, rebuilt the business after the destruction of World War II and successfully led the business until his death in 1961.

In 1962, Henkel entered into a major phase of strategic reorientation with the appointment of Konrad Henkel, Jost's younger brother, as the head of the company. When Konrad assumed the business leadership, the Henkel company employed 8,525 workers and annually produced 500,000 tons of chemical products, mainly detergents under the original brand name Persil as well as some newly launched products.

Intrigued by the growth of Henkel's direct competitor Procter & Gamble, Konrad studied their business very closely and undertook new diversification efforts, expanding the product range. In parallel, a dynamic internationalization process was started to reduce the dependence on the German home market.

Konrad also kept other family members aware of the development of the business: he instituted fortnightly information meetings with his two sisters and closely communicated with his cousins.

In the early 1980s, market conditions deteriorated with stronger foreign competitors in the European market. Worldwide overproduction of detergents led to a price war and most producers – including Henkel – started losing money for the first time.

Konrad's response was growth through acquisitions and continuing diversification. During this period, two major challenges emerged for the family:

- Continuing growth required financing during a period of high competition, lower profitability and substantial inheritance taxes
- The Henkel Group had grown substantially to nearly DM 10 billion in revenues: the role of the family as managers and owners needed to be redefined if the family did not want to become an inhibiting element.

After a lengthy reflection process, shared with his cousins and sisters, Konrad Henkel made some decisions which would dramatically influence the future role of the family.

- In 1980, Konrad stepped down as CEO and handed over executive control to a non-family manager
- A shareholders' committee was formed with family and non-family members
- In 1985, the company made an Initial Public Offering (IPO) to finance growth.

By 1996, revenue had grown to DM 16.3 billion both through organic growth and acquisitions. And the fourth and fifth generations of the Henkel family had grown to over 60 members. That year, the family members produced a new 20-year shareholder agreement which guaranteed the ongoing majority control of the family over the business. The younger generations made a clear commitment to remaining responsible majority owners and to allow the business to grow.

In 1999, the Henkel family continued to control well over 50 per cent of the voting shares and the business generated DM 21 billion in sales, of which only 23 per cent came from the original business line (detergents). The Group had over 57,000 employees, 10,000 different products and operated in 70 countries worldwide, with Germany generating 23 per cent of total revenue.

Best practices – Henkel

- Effectively managed transition of family influence
- Effective governance structures with professional guidance
- Formal visioning process for the later generational transitions
- Pooled family interests decided by each generation
- Proactive next generation development activities
- Clarity on the ownership philosophy: "business before family".

The Zegna Group

IMD Distinguished Family Business Award Winner 2000

The Zegna Group is widely considered the world leader in fine men's clothing, with a market share of 30 per cent and a yearly output of over 2 million metres of fabric, 350,000 suits, 1 million pieces of sportswear and 1.5 million ties. In 1999, group sales were around US$600 million with pretax profits of 12 per cent of sales. Total assets more than doubled from 1996 to 1999, and by 1999 the group was debt-free.

By the year 2000, the Zegna Group had 15 manufacturing plants and employed 4,500 workers, including 1,500 in Italy. With over 300 Zegna stores around the world, sales were strong in the Americas (40 per cent), Europe (40 per cent) and Asia (20 per cent).

Angelo Zegna founded Zegna in the Piedmont region of northwestern Italy. Born in 1859, the fourth child of a farmer, Angelo built a textile manufacturing plant and had a family of ten children. His sons worked in the factory, and when Angelo died in 1923, Ermenegildo, the youngest child, emerged as the next leader of the family business.

In 1930, Ermenegildo started using the latest imported English spinning machines and the name Ermenegildo Zegna became a trademark applied to the fine fabrics produced.

Ermenegildo was also an early social entrepreneur. Beginning in 1932, he started building hospitals, sports facilities, a professional training school and light, airy factories. He also built a beautiful scenic road – the Panoramica Zegna – linking the mountain villages above Trivero. Ermenegildo's children and grandchildren continue to expand this extraordinary environmental project.

Zegna began importing fabrics into the United States in 1938, selling to Italian tailors who remembered the brand. By the end of the 1930s, the company employed 1,000 workers. In 1942, the company was split into two – Ermenegildo gaining control of his flourishing business. By 1955, Ermenegildo Zegna and Sons employed 1,400 workers and their fabrics were exported to over 40 countries.

Ermenegildo's sons, Angelo, born in 1924, and his brother Aldo, born in 1920, both spent each day after school as children working in their father's factory. Following the death of Ermenegildo in 1966, Aldo and Angelo decided to expand into the manufacture of ready-made suits.

"Zegna Confection" was launched in 1968. Zegna's fabrics gave this new business enormous credibility and almost instant success. Zegna launched their first foreign plant for ready-made suits in 1973 in Spain. They opened the second foreign plant in Greece in 1975 but closed that operation two years later. Then in 1977, the Zegnas opened a plant in southern Switzerland and took their next strategic expansion step: made-to-measure men's suits.

In 1980, Zegna opened its first fully owned retail store in Paris. Five years later, they opened the next store in Milan. Many fourth-generation family members were involved in launching Zegna into retailing and dozens of new retail stores were opened around the world.

Aldo and Angelo both had four children. Paolo, born in 1956, was a son of Aldo, and Gildo, born in 1955, a son of Angelo. As their fathers had, they worked their way up in the business in different functions and emerged as the next natural leaders. In 1998, Paolo and Gildo Zegna became joint CEOs with Angelo and Aldo Zegna moving to the board. The co-CEOs are running the business as if it were a public corporation and aggressively pursuing a dynamic expansion strategy on several fronts.

The Zegna Group is a totally integrated business, controlling the entire value chain from raw materials right through to the final sale of a finished product to the customer. It is a successful business which has built on the traditions and values as defined by earlier generations but which each generation has successfully redefined and adapted to the changed world.

Best practices – Zegna

- Strong family leadership in the business
- Compelling quality-based vision
- Each generation adds entrepreneurial value: vertical integration
- Entrepreneurial risk taking and strategic experiments for the benefit of the next generation
- Strong family values defined by the early generations guiding the following generations
- Respect for environment and recognition of social responsibilities.

The Murugappa Group

IMD Distinguished Family Business Award Winner 2001

The Murugappa Group, headquartered in India, has grown from humble beginnings as the dream of a driven entrepreneur in Burma in the early 1900s. Today the conglomerate boasts revenues of US$850 million and employs 22,500 people in its 27 business units. The family traces its business history to 1760 when the great-great-great-grandfather of the founder was active in trading and money lending.

He had five sons who each, separately, built successful businesses that, in later generations, led to leadership in several industries in India.

The Group's founder was Dewan Bahadur Arunachalam Murugappa Murugappa Chettiar (known as Dewan Bahadur), the youngest of three sons, born in 1884. When Dewan Bahadur's father died, majority control of his father's estate went to the eldest son, with Dewan Bahadur receiving virtually nothing for all his work. The unfairness of this policy spurred him to divide his estate equally among his three sons – Murugappa, Vellayan and AMM. He did this while they were young men and while he was still alive to give them the freedom and the opportunity to be a family energetically pursuing business together.

In the early 1930s, Dewan Bahadur and his sons made several important decisions. They repatriated much of their investments from Burma to India so that the Great Depression, World War II and Burmese national movements didn't bankrupt the family. They also saw that India was on the verge of industrialization and took the family's first steps into major industry.

In the 1930s and 1940s, with the repatriated funds, they established a sandpaper plant (the beginning of today's US$65 million abrasives business); they purchased a steel safe manufacturing company; they started an insurance company; they bought a rubber plantation; and they created the number one bicycle company in India. The Murugappa Group was born.

Because of government regulation, it was difficult to obtain licences for new businesses. Consequently, to grow, the Murugappa Group often sought to acquire ailing units to turn around.

The most well-publicized acquisition occurred in 1981 with the purchase of EID Parry – the second oldest commercial name in India and a manufacturer of fertilizers, pesticides, confectionery and sugar. The agreement made headlines, because it showed the Group's commitment to invest in what many in India felt was a risky venture, but they saw as an opportunity to grow. EID Parry is now a business with US$265 million in sales and is 41 per cent family owned.

However, not all businesses have been a success. For example, the Group has divested a cement company, sold its electronics business and faced difficulties with its long-held construction company.

By 2001, the Group included seven substantial business units comprising 27 companies in a variety of industries. Their interests included abrasives, agro-chemicals, bicycles, chains, industrial tubes and roll forming, rubber, tea and coffee plantations, sugar mills, sanitary ware, confectionery, financial brokerage services, vehicle finance, insurance and mutual funds.

The Murugappa Group and family also continue to build on the example of philanthropy initiated by Dewan Bahadur in 1924. The family's trust, the AMM Foundation, is sustained by a fixed percentage of annual business profits and family contributions. To date it has built and nurtured four high schools of 8,000 students, a polytechnic institute of 1,000 students, four no-fee hospitals and a rural research centre.

In the late 1950s, the six third-generation sons entered the business, each rising to become managing director of one or more of the business units in the 1990s. From the late 1970s, six of seven sons in the fourth generation also joined the Group.

An important transition in organization occurred in 1985 when the Group hired, for the first time, a management consultant, AD Little, to look at issues of structure and succession. This effort resulted in a leadership succession plan. In 1996, second-generation Muru and MV both died at early ages. The family elder, AMM, urged a restructuring to improve the future of the business by relying less on family members for the day-to-day management of the business units as managing directors.

The goal of the restructuring was to introduce change without disrupting performance in an atmosphere of openness and support. The family leaders sought the help of an esteemed Indian colleague to help facilitate discussions of change among family members. To facilitate the change process, the family members on the board committed one to two days a month for almost two years. This resulted in establishing a holding company-like board and a new governance structure. The new structure was innovative for the business and for India and also brought a new perspective from the independent board members.

Best practices – Murugappa

- Strong ethical family values
- Each generation has added entrepreneurial value
- Assessment of the most effective and sustainable way for the family to add value to the business
- Creation of innovative and forward-oriented governance structures
- Efficient next-generation development process.

Samuel C. Johnson Family Enterprises

IMD Distinguished Family Business Award Winner 2002

Under Sam Johnson's (1928–2004) leadership, within just a few brief decades, the Johnson business went from a small wax company (US$171 million in sales) to four major global enterprises (combined US$8 billion in sales) that include household goods, innovative commercial products and services, environmentally responsible polymers, diverse financial services and some of the most recognized brands in the recreational industry.

Samuel Curtis Johnson (1833–1919), the original entrepreneur, sold parquet floors in his early working years. Then, in 1886, he acquired a parquet flooring business where, recognizing people's need to treat wooden floors, Johnson developed a floor wax that he mixed in a bathtub. By the turn of the century, wax sales were larger than the revenues from selling parquet floors, and soon Johnson was exporting his wax products to Britain and even Australia, and the number of employees ballooned to over 100.

In 1919, Samuel C. Johnson died, and his son, Herbert Fisk Johnson (1868–1928) inherited the business. In 1928, Herbert died unexpectedly and left the family business devoid of any will or succession plan. His son, Herbert Fisk (HF) Johnson Jr (1899–1978), assumed management control when he was 28, but it took a decade to clarify ownership.

Johnson Wax was often at the forefront in human resources policies. From 1900, it offered paid vacations to its employees. In 1917, it introduced an employee profit-sharing plan. HF established a 40-hour workweek in 1926, calling his approach "enlightened selfishness". In 1927, HF gave a speech that still serves as a philosophical guide for current generations: "The goodwill of the people is the only enduring thing in any business. It is the sole substance ... the rest is shadow."

Believing strongly in international growth, new manufacturing technologies and product quality, HF launched the "Product Plus" concept: every new Johnson product had to have a distinct advantage over everything else on the market, or it had to be new and unique enough to outstrip the competition.

In 1954, Sam joined the business as his father's assistant. He had a master's degree in business from Harvard Business School in his pocket and two years of US Air Force service. Following the advice of the consulting firm Booz, Allen and Hamilton, HF developed a career plan for Sam.

As new products director for the company, Sam developed an aerosol insecticide killer, called Raid, that met the "Product Plus" concept: It smelled better and killed insects without harming plants. The new product development process created by Sam was so innovative that it became the subject of a Harvard Business School case study. The following years saw a number of new products move the company away from wax-related products: the garden bug killer, Off (a mosquito repellent), Pledge (a furniture duster and polisher), and Glade air freshener. Within a year of market introduction, they represented 35 per cent of total domestic sales.

In 1966, at 38, Sam became President of the company, which then boasted annual sales of US$171 million. His father, HF, was honorary Chairman until his death in 1978 and remained aggressively interested in how Sam was managing the business. By 1978, Sam had built a company with revenue reaching US$1 billion, based on a strong international expansion through diversification and acquisitions.

In 1976, in a statement of corporate philosophy entitled "This We Believe", Sam codified the basic principles that drove the family business. To these Sam added: "The way of safeguarding these beliefs is to remain a privately held company. Our way of reinforcing them is to make profits through growth and development, profits which allow us to do more for all the people on whom we depend."

Sam had four children – Curt, Fisk, Helen and Winnie, all four of whom joined the company. Sam undertook a widely publicized trip to Brazil with his sons following in the tracks of his father. By 1998, the family had created a council that became the forum for succession planning, preparing next-generation family members and creating a large degree of transparency. Sam, who had seen many family businesses suffer from sibling rivalry, wanted to avoid siblings reporting to each other. In 1999, the family arrived at a suitable arrangement: Fisk became chairman of SC Johnson, the core consumer products business; Helen became chairman of Johnson Outdoors Inc., the recreational products business; Curt became chairman of JohnsonDiversey, then the second largest institutional and industrial products and services business in the world; and Winnie, who had a lesser interest in the business, became president of the Johnson Family Foundation.

Best practices – Johnson

- Highly entrepreneurial spirit in each generation
- Business must produce products which are unique or offer a distinctive advantage
- Strong values based business principles
- Deep respect for the environment and the community.

The Bonnier Group

2003 IMD-Lombard Odier Darier Hentsch Distinguished Family Business Award Winner

The Bonnier Group is a leading Scandinavian diversified-media conglomerate of over 200 privately owned companies. The ownership is in the hands of 73 family members from the fifth to the eighth generations who are direct descendants of the founding family.

The Bonnier family business began in 1804 when Gerhard Bonnier (1778–1862), the founder and son of a banker in Dresden, opened a library in Copenhagen. He grew his modest library into a book publishing business. His youngest son, Albert, opened his own Stockholm publishing firm in 1837, called Albert Bonniers Förlag, which became the platform for today's media group. From his profits, Albert invested in a printing house and then in *Dagens Nyheter*, a leading Swedish daily newspaper. After Albert's death in 1900, his son Karl Otto took the company into daily papers and magazines – taking a controlling interest in *Dagens Nyheter*, then the largest daily newspaper in Sweden.

In the fourth generation, at Karl Otto's death, business ownership went to three of his sons Tor, Åke and Kaj. Karl Otto's first son, Tor (1883–1976), assumed both business and family leadership. In 1929, Tor acquired the magazine publishing firm Åhlen & Åkerlund. It was a big risk: the price equalled the approximate value of the family business. Until then, the Bonnier businesses had grown organically or through self-financed investments.

In 1952, Kaj was bought out by Tor and Åke, leaving two owners in the fourth generation. In the fifth generation the family business had seven owners with very unequal shareholdings. To gain clarity and commitment, they signed a 50-year ownership contract.

In the fifth generation, Abbe Bonnier emerged as the leader, with a strong entrepreneurial drive. Abbe launched a daily evening newspaper and adopted a 30-year strategy of self-financed unrelated diversification and expansion. The Group made initial investments in vertically related industries like paper. Increasingly, though, Abbe acquired companies in unrelated industries like furniture production, disposable tableware, packaging, engineering and ferry services.

In 1976, a profitable new financial paper was launched: *Dagens Industri*. Then in 1978, Abbe stepped up from working President to working Chairman of the Group, and a non-family outsider was chosen as President.

The seven male Bonnier descendants and owners in Abbe's fifth generation evolved to 28 descendants (of both genders) in the sixth generation. Carl-Johan, the third son of Abbe's brother Johan, became the next-generation leader as CEO in 1991. Born in 1951, Carl-Johan had entered the family business right after his university graduation.

The sixth generation concluded that it should focus on the traditional industry – media – and capitalize on new opportunities there. To fund this strategy, there were divestitures of investments in unrelated industries. In 1998, Bonnier acquired Marieberg, a publicly traded publishing business, and merged it into the Bonnier Group (still 100 per cent privately owned). Marieberg cost close to €500 million – about half of the Bonnier Group's assets at the time. At the same time the Bonniers developed a new approach to governance of their business and family interests and the family unanimously signed a new shareholder agreement valid until 2030. In 2003, 12 family members were working at different levels in the Group.

As the Bonnier Group celebrates its 200th anniversary, the sixth and seventh generations appear to be firmly committed to the future as a family business. The Group has governance structures in place – both for the business and for the family – that they use actively and to ensure transparency, commitment and emotional attachment to the business.

Best practices – Bonnier

- Strong family culture and cohesion
- Family and business identity closely interlinked
- Strong communication culture within the family
- Evolving, highly structured and effective family and business governance
- Explicit and transparent family ownership philosophy
- Each generation freely renews the commitment to the business.

The Barilla Group

2004 IMD-Lombard Odier Darier Hentsch Distinguished Family Business Award Winner

The Barilla Group is not only the largest Italian food processing business but also the world market leader for pasta products.

In 1877, Pietro Barilla, then in his twenties, opened a bakery shop in the centre of Parma, Italy, where he sold bread and pasta. In 1910, the first factory was built, employing 80 workers. His sons Riccardo and Gualtiero had worked alongside their father since they were 14 years old. In 1919, Gualtiero died suddenly.

Riccardo, with the help of his wife Virginia and his two sons Pietro and Gianni, continued to invest. By 1936, 700 workers were producing 80 tons of pasta and 15 tons of bread per day using six continuous presses. As in the previous generation, the functional responsibilities were split into technical (Gianni) and commercial (Pietro). The problems started when Pietro, the more entrepreneurially oriented of the two brothers, was drafted into military service in 1939 and sent to the Russian front. Air raids also damaged part of the plant.

When he returned from the war, Pietro and his brother Gianni started to rebuild the business. In 1950, Pietro visited the United States to study American marketing practices. As a result, they stopped bread production in 1952 in order to focus exclusively on pasta. In 1955, Barilla was the first manufacturer to pack pasta in portion-sized cardboard boxes. The consumer market was growing again. By 1960, there were 1,300 workers and a sales team of 200. In 1969, the company built the world's largest pasta manufacturing plant in Pedrignano.

The completion of the plant coincided with one of Italy's darkest periods. Political and social unrest grew. A spate of terrorism with almost daily victims and kidnappings created uncertainty and unrest. Gianni Barilla felt that they should sell the business and leave the country, but Pietro wanted none of that. Gianni, who held 50 per cent of the business, offered his share to Pietro, but Pietro could not buy his brother out. In 1971, the 94-year-old family business was sold to the US multinational Grace, which wanted to enter the food market in Italy.

By 1979, the company had sales of €130 million and employed 1,600 people. But Grace was not satisfied with its entry into the Italian food market and put the company up for sale. Pietro Barilla, who had never given up hope of regaining ownership, worked feverishly to raise the necessary capital. Finally, he succeeded in buying back the company from the US multinational. Pietro was 66 years old in 1979, but appeared to have boundless energy and a strong period of growth started. In 1993, at the age of 80, Pietro Barilla died, leaving a €2 billion company to his four children.

When their father died, the siblings made it clear that they would jointly continue to develop the family business according to the entrepreneurial spirit of the previous three generations. But they also wanted to introduce new ways of managing the growing business. To support the professionalization process, the brothers brought in a former Procter & Gamble CEO. Just three years after market entry, Barilla was market leader for pasta in the US. Many innovations, acquisitions and upgradings took place. A particularly remarkable move was the acquisition of the German Kamps Group in 2002.

The brothers' governance philosophy is: "Influence but don't interfere." In addition to their ownership role on the different boards, they are present in three key committees. They have made it clear that they will never sell the company or go public.

Best practices – Barilla

- Emotional ownership as a key motivator for strong entrepreneurial growth
- Strong family values based on personal discipline
- Clarity of the role of the family in the business through evolving governance structures – "Influence but don't interfere"

- Each generation builds on the achievements of the preceding generation
- Generational inspiration and clarity of focus through the founder's vision.

2
Threats to Multigenerational Survival of Family Businesses

Growing any business is a challenge. Growing a family business is even more of a challenge as evidenced by the fact that a vast majority of small- to medium-sized family businesses grow very little. In order to support a growing, multigenerational family, its leaders must adopt growth as both a mindset and as an objective to be implemented over time. There are three reasons for this. Firstly, as the family grows there are exponentially more family owners and that translates into paying a growing number of dividends. Secondly, market conditions change and adaptation and renewal are necessary. Few family businesses escape the need to adapt. Business growth is the outward sign of successful adaptation and responding to market needs. Thirdly, when business growth is built upon a vision that each successive generation has developed and implemented, it confirms a sense of personal worth and professional achievement for the family and its leaders. Instead of just inheriting a business and its already existing vision, the successor generation is seen as contributors in their own right – leaders who have developed their own vision. This positive perception is held both by themselves and by others, including non-management family members and the organization's management and employees.

The next generation leaders need to be seen and recognized as entrepreneurs, in their own right, and as a really powerful engine for business growth in the family business. Most successors attempt to obtain this recognition as fast as possible by focusing on business strategies before having transitioned through a phased development process. Best practices from the most successful family businesses highlight that business growth should be wisely constructed on previous generations' achievements and not undertaken needlessly at any cost. Particularly for family businesses, which are mindful of their tradition, evolutionary growth usually is more effective in the long term than revolutionary growth.

The three family business archetypes

Over a very long-term view, there are three typical family business archetypes:

- Ephemeral family business
- Preserving family business
- Entrepreneurial family business.

After describing the different three archetypes, this book focuses on successful "entrepreneurial family business".

Ephemeral family business

The ephemeral family business is typically a single-generation business or a business which fails during the early stages of the second generation. Its success is dependent upon one strong entrepreneur. It is a "me" business: the company truly is an extension of the entrepreneur, and it lacks the systematic base to shift from a "me" to an "us" business; this is the key requirement for an effective family business. It may be labelled a family business because several family members may be active alongside – or under – the entrepreneur. But if a vision and an effective system for a subsequent generation's ownership are not in place, it fails to qualify as a successful multigenerational family business. Most businesses started up by an entrepreneur follow this model. These are not necessarily small businesses: a recent example of such a case is Parmalat in Italy, where the lack of a sustainable, values-based vision by the founder drove the company into bankruptcy in 2003.

Preserving family business

This type of family business may have survived over several or even a large number of generations, but it suffers from constraints which allow little or no growth. Typical examples of the preserving family business are family farms and vineyards: Tradition implies that the first-born male descendant assumes ownership and leadership. A conservative culture leads to a preserving, rather than a growth, view. Fixed assets are often physically limited and not conducive to business growth. The implication for a family growing over multiple generations is that the family has to adapt to the business constraints. This adaptation implies personal sacrifices as each generation needs to go through an enforced – or increasingly voluntary – selection process. Traditionally these sacrifices are associated with both financial and emotional costs for the departing family members.

Entrepreneurial family business

An entrepreneurial family business has a very different vision from the ones described above. Rather than simplifying structures as in the "preserving family business" or having no structure as in the "ephemeral family business", they embrace complexity based on families growing over multiple generations. Instead of excluding family members, they research inclusive structures and strategies which can address the diverse needs of the growing family. Growing families experience diversity on many levels, including interests and competence. The underlying vision is that all individual family members benefit from keeping the family business together, because the structures and strategies that are adopted constructively address the diverse needs of all constituencies. However, aligning these needs must be done in a way which respects the egalitarian culture of the family on one side and the meritocratic culture of the business on the other side. In addition, the family members that choose to stay together explicitly or implicitly subscribe to a spirit of growth; the business needs to grow in order to be able to satisfy the needs of a growing family.

This book focuses on the strategies adopted by the award-winning companies which belong to the archetype of the "entrepreneurial family businesses". There is something noble about this archetype: it is the answer to those critics who see no future for family businesses. The nine award-winning family businesses analysed for this book show variations of this archetype and how, over time, each generation created their own balanced system of complex relationships between the closely connected constituencies which are unique to family business: family, ownership, management and the individual. It is the archetype of the "entrepreneurial family business" which best reinforces the strengths of family businesses while acknowledging – and accommodating – their potential weaknesses. An example of a weakness of fundamental importance, which almost all family businesses face over time, is the diverging interests and values of growing families. When families disagree about ownership and management strategy, they are forced to face the issue of splitting. The award-winning family businesses provide many examples of "pruning the family tree". In most cases, pruning was accomplished with a sense of pain. However, over time, those family members who committed themselves to continuing together as family business owners appeared to emerge with a refreshed, energized focus on future growth strategies for the business.

Is the family a threat to survival?

An understanding of the role of family can be gained by comparing family businesses with other forms of corporate organizations. The essential differences lie in both the proximity and the identity of the shareholders. In a widely held public corporation, ownership is typically very fragmented and heterogeneous, whereas shareholders in a family business are much closer to the business. In addition, the shareholder belongs to a clearly defined entity – "the family".

Both proximity and identity have potentially huge implications for the business. A greater need for consensus/stability (and rigidity) of ownership in a family business is an issue for both owners and managers, since it is much more difficult for shareholders to "vote with their feet" – that is, to sell shares and walk away if they disagree with other family members.

Shareholder proximity

On the positive side, having shareholders who are close to the business implies they have a better understanding of the business. If this understanding addresses the needs of the business, it can provide a powerful added value to the business. And it is in the interest of the shareholders to maximize the financial value of their shares. Leveraging shareholder proximity in effective ways is one of the common traits of successful multigenerational family businesses. The award-winning family businesses in this book are all strong examples of this strategy. On the negative side, shareholder proximity provides the potential for "meddling" in the business and thus not respecting the boundaries between ownership and management rights and responsibilities. Another consequence of proximity, which can be potentially damaging for the business, is the possibility of putting excessive focus on "milking the business" financially.

Shareholder identity

Shareholder identity: this is clearly the family! When the family first starts the business, identity is strong and homogeneous. The founder, that is the entrepreneur, is not only very visible but also carries the personal and family culture – as expressed by the values – into the business. The homogeneity of one family remains intact if, over generations, the ownership base remains very narrow. This is typically the case in both the owner-manager and dominant owner structures where, frequently, other family branches are "pruned" or bought out in order to retain a small ownership base.

The other contrasting option is allowing a growing number of family owners in each generation. One example is the Bonnier family where, in 2003, a total of 73 family members from the fifth to the eighth generation share ownership.

Typically, in the latter structure, retaining family homogeneity becomes an issue that needs to be addressed if the family wants to stay united as business owners. Over multiple generations, the addition of in-laws, the emergence of diverse personal interests and the eventual geographic dispersion of family members creates a natural centrifugal force negatively impacting the family commonalities. Therefore, over time, older and larger families tend to naturally become more heterogeneous. This is when the following question needs to be addressed: "Why continue as a family business?"

Family shareholders differentiate themselves from anonymous shareholders in public corporations, because they are emotionally attached to the business. Most family businesses fail to see this from the perspective of an inherent strength that is something which can be leveraged both for the benefit of the business and the family. The award-winning family businesses in this book are examples of families that create a vision which constructively integrates both the needs of growing businesses and growing families.

The family identity provides the stakeholders with a reference point on business, financial and values aspects. This clearly implies a responsibility for the family to understand and meet these expectations.

Table 2.1 Family: opportunity and threat for the business

	Proximity	Identity
Opportunity	• In-depth and historic knowledge of the business: "institutional memory" • Strongest interest in financial success of the business	• Tangible forms of reference, including "the buck stops here" • The values enacted by the family
Threat	• Not qualified and competent to understand the business • The financial interest too individually biased: "Milking the business"	• The family identity limiting business opportunities • The values not being supportive of the business

The proximity and the identity of the family to its business represent both the greatest opportunities and the greatest threats for family businesses (see Table 2.1). The linkages between family and business have the potential to create "grey" areas of confusion – both for insiders and outsiders. They require that effective communication structures be put in place in order to deal with these issues and create cohesion and consensus.

The greatest need for clarity on the family and business linkages arises before, during and after generational transitions.

The most important threat to survival: general transitions

The arrival of a new leadership generation is, without doubt, the most critical time for any family business, irrespective of size, strategic circumstances or performance. Transitions upset the equilibrium that has worked efficiently for each of the four dimensions of the family business system: family, ownership, management and each individual. This equilibrium typically tends to follow the family's generational pattern: each generation of family members define their vision for ownership. This then impacts its management strategy and the opportunity for the individual member to play a certain role within the family business. The definition of this vision is either explicit or implicit leading to the emergence of a framework for all stakeholders to operate within and to set their expectations. Non-family business leaders require clarity on the ownership's expectations, and those, in turn, are dependent on the family's intentions. It is usually in the interest of the business leader to maintain a clearly defined and balanced equilibrium among these four dimensions for as long as possible. This enables the leader to focus attention on management leadership issues.

As mentioned above, the arrival of a next-generation leader significantly impacts this equilibrium along each of the four dimensions. The family is confronted with a changing intergenerational relationship which shifts from "parent–child" to "adult–adult". Ownership is brought to the forefront as the next generation considers and experiences the impact of ownership control. Management is significantly impacted by the arrival of a new generation with their differences in education and experience levels from the outgoing generation. Each individual – outgoing and incoming generations alike – is impacted by differences resulting from their respective lifecycle stages. Therefore, the equilibrium, as established by the outgoing generation, undergoes system-wide changes when the next generation leader arrives.

Leadership succession in a family business is also considerably more complex than in the widely held public corporation, mainly due to the following three factors:

1. Family businesses need to consider the real impact of ownership, both in terms of identity and proximity. As mentioned earlier, ownership is in the hands of a family and, therefore, not anonymous and not as easily transferable. The family has clearly defined its identity and ownership objectives. These typically differ from those of anonymous shareholders in a public corporation, where they tend to be more short-term oriented and more volatile. In addition, the family is close to the business. It brings both a broad and a deep understanding of the company and an institutional memory, both of which are lacking in a public corporation.
2. Leadership succession in a family business is typically between related persons, such as from father to son. This family relationship adds an element of complexity that results in both weaknesses and strengths.
3. The typical leadership tenure in a family business is long: a working life. The tenure range often varies from not less than one decade to thirty or forty years. In larger public corporations, research points to dramatically shorter tenure periods for CEOs.

What does this mean for the next-generation leader in a family business?

The strong linkage of family and business over a long time horizon has unique implications for the successor in a family business. First and foremost, there is the strong identity of the outgoing leader. One individual, whose tenure has lasted several decades, leaves an indelible imprint on how the business is managed. The reference point for "the way things are done around here" is the one person who has led the business for such a long time. The implication for the successor is immensely important, because the culture of the entire organization is characterized by the personality of the predecessor. The positive aspect to a long tenure is that there is a familiarity with the decision-making process and how things are done.

However, the negative aspect to familiarity is that any attempt to change by the successor will directly reflect on any previous decisions made by the predecessor. Therefore, the potential for intergenerational conflicts is enormous. And change, particularly from the perspective of a successor who arrives with new educational knowledge and new ideas, may be overdue in a business that has been led by one individual over several decades. Indeed, a very long-term leadership tenure harbours the risk of focusing too much on historically proven products and processes at the expense of innovation. Often, the perception of a next-generation successor entering the family business is that there is too much historic orientation and that a more forward-oriented strategy should be adopted.

In summary, the challenges for a successor entering the family business are multiple, and they face issues that are fundamental in nature:

- A business culture defined by one individual
- A business strategy adapted to the experiences of the outgoing leader
- A parent–child relationship between the outgoing and the incoming leader.

The significance of these challenges is such that they typically lead to conflicts between the generations and other stakeholders. The vast majority of family businesses are either unprepared or ill-prepared to comprehensively and effectively address these challenges. Research data from several countries confirm that less than one quarter of family businesses have an explicit, written succession plan (IMD-Lombard Odier Family Business Center, 2001). The lack of a comprehensive plan to prepare for the next-generation leadership succession, and to consider the impact on the family, the individual, the ownership and the management needs, considerably increases the risks of failure for the successor as we will see below.

The risk of failure is very real

The opportunity costs resulting from an ineffective handling of the successor's challenges can be as high as the total failure of the family business. One very visible and highly publicized example is the Swiss-based André Trading Group, which went bankrupt in 2001. The André Group was known as one of the "five sisters" of world grain trading. It was founded in 1877 and imported grain and other food products. It was under the leadership of third-generation Georges André that the business experienced strong international growth mainly in grain, cocoa, coffee and rice trading in Latin America, Africa, Asia and the now former communist countries. In the 1980s, the company was active in 70 countries with revenues said to exceed US$10 billion. In the 1990s, the changing environment started to negatively affect the André Group: the emergence of the internet brought transparency, and companies could directly access the market, thus reducing the role of the traditional trader. Furthermore, the communist trading bloc collapsed. The André family had always been intensely private and unwilling to become more transparent. When fourth-generation Henri André formally became chairman, his predecessor, Georges André, continued to maintain his authority well into the mid-1990s. Henri, who had wanted to become an architect, had entered the family's business and accepted the chairman's role out of obligation to the family. Due to an emotional father–son relationship and the continued involvement of his father, he found it difficult to introduce much-needed change. In March 2001, after a period of rapid deterioration and heavy losses, the company had to file for bankruptcy protection. The local press blamed the failure on inadequate succession planning (Vermot, 2001: 8).

What are the real challenges for next-generation leaders?

Identifying reasons why family businesses fail following a succession invariably brings out comments like: "The successor did not have the same business leadership competence as the father." The reason for failure is naturally attributed to the successor, because failure occurred during his tenure. However, a deeper analysis is required: the successor's cited lack of business leadership competence normally only represents the tip of the iceberg and is a symptom not the root cause. Usually, the true cause is much deeper and more complex. Further light is shed on this by Henri André, 62, the last chairman of the failed André Trading Group:

> I could not address some of the real and fundamental problems of the business, because this would have meant overturning key decisions taken by the previous leaders to whom I am particularly close: my father and my uncle. For my father, restructuring would have meant abandoning everything that he and his father had built up. (Grant and Roberts, 2001: 38)

This is an insightful statement by the leader of a failed family business. It implies that he perceived and understood the need for business changes, but family relationships prevented these necessary decisions from being made and implemented. These emotionally driven family relationships restricted the individual, the next-generation successor, to introduce management changes which could have positively impacted the ownership, and subsequently the family and the individual dimensions. The fundamental differences between family businesses and widely held public corporations clearly emerge here. A new CEO in a public corporation can fully disregard the impact that change would have on the credibility and character of the predecessor. In fact, this has become a broadly applied business practice in public corporations since discrediting allows a new leader to blame past leaders for current problems and create financial reserves which will predictably benefit the coming periods. Furthermore, general management education and practice fails to be a useful guide for the particular dilemmas that family successors face. The typical recommendations given to successors in widely owned corporations are to:

- Focus on the future
- Break with the past by overturning decisions made by the predecessor.

The most visible and continually most profitable and most researched large public corporation is, undoubtedly, General Electric in the US. In 1981, the outgoing CEO, Reginald Jones, advised his successor on the best approach for the future: "Blow it up." The name of the successor was Jack Welch, who then changed the fundamental strategies of his predecessor and led GE to outstanding success, predominantly through acquisitions. Twenty years later, Jack Welch, in turn, advised his successor, Jeffery Immelt, to again "blow it up". Since 2001, Immelt is actively overturning the acquisitions-based strategy of his much-lauded predecessor by preaching internal growth (Useem, 2004: 40–7).

This example emphasizes the typical successor's paradigm: "Assert yourself quickly through new strategies for the business." While this philosophy is visibly applied in widely held corporations in need of meeting ever higher shareholder expectations, successors in family businesses also tend to adopt this approach. However, they do so for different reasons. The fundamental reason is not shareholder driven, but rather, it relates mainly to the leader's need to be accepted as a competent leader by the predecessor, usually the father, as well as by the rest of the family, non-family management and the business' employees. This challenge is unique to family businesses. This uniqueness is expressed by the existence of the four levels of interest found only in family businesses: family, ownership, management and the individual.

Each of these levels defines distinct areas of interest that interact with each other. In a widely held corporation, the business is steered by management, because ownership is widely dispersed. By contrast, in the family business, it is the family that defines the ownership strategy that, in turn, drives the business. The next-generation successor, as an individual, is subjected to the constraints set by the four different interest levels. For leadership to be successful, a carefully balanced approach recognizes and understands how the distinct interest levels interact with each other and also change over time. Effective family business leadership attempts to create and adapt equilibrium amongst the dynamic needs of the four interest levels. As mentioned in the Introduction, the potential for conflict is high and increases at the time of a generational succession. In addition, over the lifetime of the successor, this equilibrium needs to be modified multiple times, responding to both internal and external changes. Internal changes are often predictable since they are based on human lifecycle phases, whereas the external changes are less predictable due to a higher degree of complexity.

3
Understanding the Family Business Leadership Challenges

Generational transitions are the most critical periods for any multigenerational family business. The functioning equilibrium of the stakeholders' four needs – family, ownership, management and the individual – is upset and a new equilibrium needs to be found in order to provide stability and transparency for the overall system. There are, however, inherent weaknesses in the system which tend to add complications in reaching a new and functioning equilibrium as quickly as possible. Quite the opposite, these weaknesses, as I outline below, tend to favour the creation of conflicts, most typically between two generations.

- **Weakness 1: lack of experience in generational transitioning**
  Succession is a rare event. For the founding generation, there simply is no internal benchmark, because they only experience it once – when they have to let go. Subsequent generations experience succession only two times – when they enter the family business and when they then exit it. The fact that these are rare events gives them an extraordinary character with a high level of insecurity. Furthermore, a succession that one has "lived through" is not necessarily helpful in providing meaningful guidelines when planning the next succession. This is particularly relevant when the family business undergoes a cultural shift from one generation to the next due to growth

in the number of next-generation family members. Applying the benchmark of an "I" culture, marked by a single dominant owner-manager, to an "us" culture, made up of a team of next-generation siblings, is simply counter-productive. The same can be said for the transition from an "us" to an "us and them" culture, which occurs when a family grows to a size where members experience different interests and needs. Therefore, each succession has its own structural requirements and characteristics which are fundamentally determined by present and, more importantly, future needs.

- **Weakness 2: increasing role confusion**
  The arrival of a next generation in the family business is a time of uncertainty for both generations. Communication and exchange of information is increasingly needed. Over time, discussions between parents and children address ownership and management issues which add new complexities. This requires an adaptation, as the usual family-driven content of communication is now increased by ownership and management content. It is now necessary to distinguish between the different interest levels of family, ownership, management and the individual when information is sent and when it is received. The junior generation often feels confused by a lack of experience and understanding of which role the parent generation adopts when messages are transmitted. In particular, negative information that is transmitted from the senior to the junior generation tends to create a strain on relationships if it is unclear which interest level it is intended to address. For both generations, this requires an adaptation and learning period on how to best avoid role confusion.

- **Weakness 3: an unadapted intergenerational communication style**
  The communication style between both generations also undergoes change, often fluctuating. From the traditional

and dominant parent–child communication style, it needs to be brought in alignment with an adult–adult relationship as the content of the communication shifts to more ownership and management related issues. Family members are typically not effective communicators amongst themselves due to communication patterns that are formed early and then maintained. As the nature of the relationship between the generations evolves to adult–adult, the communication style tends to experience a time lag in adapting to the needs of a more business and rational, as opposed to emotional, exchange of information. Particularly in times of difficult circumstances – such as succession – the communication style tends to fluctuate frequently, thereby causing confusion, mixed messages and further increasing the potential for conflict.

What do they want?

The three inherent system weaknesses in handling succession are further exacerbated by the respective mindsets of the outgoing and incoming generations. IMD research has clearly identified that both generations approach the issues around succession with highly ineffective mindsets.

For several years, during the public IMD programme "Leading the Family Business" as well as a large number of private programmes, one key assignment separated the participants into two groups – the outgoing generation and the incoming generation. Each group was asked to list their respective recommendations to the other generation on how to facilitate succession. For many participants, this was the first chance they had to formally reflect upon and recognize the needs of the other generation. In addition, considering the question in a peer group enhances the breadth and the depth of the identified issues. The following lists are a collection of the typical recommendations, based on the same exercise conducted with over a dozen different groups (Schwass, 2005).

Typical advice from the outgoing to the incoming generation on "how to facilitate succession"

- Seek a good education and complete it
- Gain outside experience
- Start at the bottom
- Learn about all details in the business
- Choose the best employees – more intelligent than yourself – if possible
- Understand your obligation towards your family
- Be proud of your family
- Don't expect us to make decisions for you.

Typical advice from the incoming to the outgoing generation on "how to facilitate succession"

- Plan early for transition
- Find other activities to fill your time
- Arrange practical issues: tax and financial planning
- Clear up unresolved issues
- Plan how to introduce new family members to the business
- Give shares early
- Create business governance structure
- Create family governance structure
- Be clear about your intentions/wishes/interests to the family and management
- Accept that change is necessary
- Assure your own economic independence
- Be open to the idea of an outside facilitator
- Let go!

What do these lists tell us?

As I hinted at earlier, these lists – which have shown few substantial variations from group to group through the years – reveal surprising consistency and overlap in both the communication styles and the mindsets, as applied by each generation. Clearly, the communication style is based on a parent–child relationship. The outgoing generation tells the next generation somewhat authoritatively what to do. The incoming generation, on the other hand, requests clarity and preparation. Both reflect typical parent–child behavioural roles.

There is equal consistency in the mindsets of each generation. Very clearly both are "I" or "me" based. Each generation expects the other to undertake initiatives for the benefit of the other. This is most evident when the incoming generation tells the outgoing to withdraw from the family business, "Give shares early" and "Let go!"

Therefore, these lists appear to indicate that neither generation is adopting the most constructive, forward-oriented approach towards managing successor issues. Neither the parent–child communication style, nor the "I" based mindsets are conducive to jointly constructing the future. This apparent deadlock between generations needs to be broken.

The change initiative

> "You must be the change you want to see in the world."
> Gandhi

During succession, intergenerational relationships frequently fluctuate between the historic parent–child and a more future-oriented, adult–adult style. This certainly applies to the majority of successions that occur in a direct line from parents to children. These fluctuations cause insecurity and anxiety, particularly for the incoming generation whose objective is to assert themselves both personally and professionally. Because the outgoing generation is already in the adult role, it is clearly the incoming generation who has the most to gain by pressing for a rapid evolution from the child to the adult stage. This, however, requires a fundamental cultural shift by overthrowing the historic parent–child relationship. A "bottom up" initiative by the next generation can typically be perceived by the parent generation as an act of protest and revolution against an established order and system – disrupting the family relationship equilibrium. The most frequent approach is an extended period of trial and error, where the next generation tests out new boundaries, which are often rebuffed by the senior generation. The fundamental nature of this intergenerational exchange is that of opponents: "you versus me". This implies a "win–lose" situation that hurts the family harmony.

Family harmony requires a culture of trust and respect that is easier to achieve within the framework of a "win–win" situation. For both generations to win, the most effective approach is to create a forward-looking perspective, which provides tangible and intangible gains for both generations. Insights into best practices of the most successful family businesses point towards an unconventional "bottom up" initiative by the next generation. The incoming generation desires change and, therefore, is the biggest beneficiary of a successful initiative. But for this "I" initiative to succeed it must target an "us" objective where both generations benefit in meaningful ways over time.

Transition is evolution – not revolution

This chapter analyses the next-generation leadership challenges according to the four different interest levels and how they evolve over time. Adding time as an additional component to this analysis is relevant mainly for two reasons. Firstly, human life is not linear but evolves though a series of phases with potentially changing needs and interests. The resulting predictability allows a better understanding of and planning for these changes. Secondly, in family businesses, the concept of "successor" tends to remain alive for a considerably longer time period than in a widely held public corporation. The reasons are the continuity in terms of ownership and the proximity to several generations of family members who tend to keep the memory of the outgoing generation alive. Even management and other employees tend to refer to successors as "young" or address them on a first-name basis in order to differentiate them from the earlier generation.

While the label of "successor" often stays for decades, the underlying responsibilities evolve and along with them, the needs and interests of the successor.

Adding the time component helps successors keep track of the natural evolution. The model tracking the evolution through time, as shown in Figure 3.1, is based on three main leadership phases from the perspective of the full lifecycle of a successor from entering until leaving the family business: "do", "lead to do" and "let do".

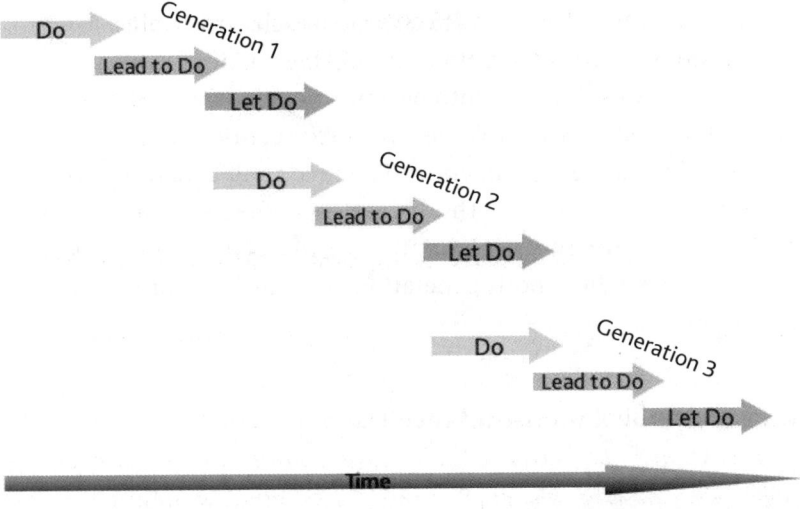

Figure 3.1 Generational leadership cycle

The "do" phase covers the beginning period of a successor actively working in the family business. Typically, this is in a lower hierarchy position with the clear objective of learning and understanding the business. The "lead to do" phase starts with the promotion of the successor to the leadership role with clearly defined authority and responsibilities. Finally, the "let do" phase covers the retirement of the successor, overlapping with the "do" phase of the following generation of successors who, in turn, experience the same cycle.

Usually, successors entering the family business do not perceive and conceptualize successor leadership as a sequential multiphase process. Their mental reference point and objective for the role of a successor is the "lead to do" phase. Due to the long tenure times of family business leaders, often the next generation has not experienced and lived through their parent's "do" phase and therefore set their expectations and entitlements intuitively – and prematurely – at the "lead to do" phase. These expectations, if realized, would cause the successor to miss out on experiencing the "do" phase before progressing to the next phase. It is the earlier "do" phase which provides the experience or the hands-on knowledge, learning and commitment to personal individual growth before exercising leadership authority. A proactive career development plan supports the growing leadership role in the business. The "lead to do" phase sees the growth of the business and a preparation for a new future governance role in the "let do" phase.

To summarize, family businesses are particularly vulnerable around the period of generational transition. This is due to system-inherent weaknesses which, if unaddressed, increase the potential for intergenerational conflict. Leadership transition in the family business is an evolutionary process that, over time, has to address the needs of the family and the ownership, beyond the management's and the individual's needs. The following analysis looks at the successor's leadership challenges both in terms of the three sequential phases and the interacting four different constituent interest levels. Finally, a matrix summarizes the challenges throughout the three phases.

The "do" phase

This phase covers the starting period of the successor in the family business. Typically, employment is at an entry management level, which can vary from a lower to higher level, depending on the successor's age, experience and the objectives of the family.

The challenges the successor faces within this phase can be analysed according to the interest levels: family, ownership, management, individual.

Family

Typically, the influence of the family remains strong during the "do" phase. This is mainly age related since the common age bracket of the successor in this phase tends to be 25–35 years.

The family influence is also process related: active communication takes place between both generations in regards to the new appointment and its implications for the various family members. The successor's key challenge, associated with family, is the nature of the relationship between both generations. In this phase, it typically oscillates between a parent–child and an adult–adult relationship. Both generations struggle with moving from the first to the second. The senior generation tends to favour the parent–child relationship, while the successor attempts to evolve to an adult–adult relationship. Usually, in periods of intergenerational conflict, the parent–child relationship tends to prevail; this can lead to complete communication blockages.

Ownership

During the "do" phase, the successor's ownership interest challenge relates to the uncertainty on access to ownership. The parent generation typically sees no interest in addressing the issue of a potential future transfer of ownership to the next generation and prefers to keep their options open for a number of reasons. Some are related to the uncertainty about the competence and commitment of the next-generation successor. In other cases, if there are several children in the next generation, the parents may want to keep the options open for another successor, at a later point. They may not know how to effectively pass on ownership to the next generation if one is the active leader and others are not involved in the business. Or they may simply perceive ownership as a vehicle to control the business and the next generation. The perspective of the next generation on ownership is initially in a waiting mode, trusting the parents to address – sometime later – this issue in the right and fair way and, for now, leaving the control to the parents.

Management

During the "do" phase, the challenges for the successor, who originates from the management level, are about finding the right place in the business. It is also a period of uncertainty about this level: the successor attempts to find the appropriate balance between, on one hand, personal aspirations and professional competence, and, on the other hand, the business' needs. The objective is to gain outside approval and recognition as a competent manager, while simultaneously navigating through a difficult learning process. The successors know that they are under particularly close observation by virtually everybody surrounding them – their family, other owners, non-family management and employees – all are carefully watching to find out if and how the successor matches up to the predecessor. This "fish-bowl" culture puts a particular strain on the behaviour and attitude of the successor.

Individual

The "do" phase from the individual perspective is characterized as a period of learning, testing and uncertainty. The horizon is short-term as the focus is on rapidly reaching a platform of independence from the family and recognition within the business. The prevailing motivation is largely around "safety" needs, both financial and psychological. In this phase, the mindset tends to be set on the individual and their personal needs, and less on those of the others. The individual challenge is in developing **personal** leadership. It is in the "do" phase that a structured and explicit approach to growing as an individual and growing the role in the business is critical for the transitioning to the leadership position in the "lead to do" phase, both for reasons of inner strengthening and recognition by others.

The successor's challenges by interest level in the "do" phase can therefore be summarized as shown in Table 3.1.

The "lead to do" phase

The "lead to do" phase starts when the successor is promoted to a clearly defined leadership position in the family business. This

Table 3.1 The successor's challenges by interest level in the "do" phase

Phase \ Interests	Family	Ownership	Management	Individual
Do	Child–parent relationship	Control dependent	Professional assertion	Personal leadership

involves setting higher hierarchical and strategy responsibilities. This step usually occurs when the successor is in the 35–50 age range. The challenges faced by the successor in this phase are analysed according to the four interest levels: family, ownership, management and individual.

Family

In the "lead to do" phase the relationship between the successor and the parent generation undergoes fundamental changes. One determining factor is the advancing individualization process of the successor, that is, the successor is gaining both personal and professional independence. Another key factor is the creation of a new nuclear family with the successor getting married and having children. As the intergenerational distance increases, the parent generation may feel that the separation process is a painful one. In this phase, the prevailing parent–child relationship increasingly shifts to an adult–adult relationship. This relationship transition is often the result of conflicting intergenerational situations arising from business-related power struggles between the outgoing and incoming leaders. The "lead to do" phase is essentially characterized by a growing distance between the generations that significantly increases the potential for conflicts and thereby increases the successor's challenges.

Ownership

The "lead to do" phase is marked by a struggle for ownership control. The parent generation, experiencing a loss of influence over the next generation – both on the family and the management levels – sees ownership as the last remaining vehicle to exercise effective control over the successor. Frequently, the successor considers the alternative of staying versus leaving the family business. The feeling usually experienced by the successor is that it is unfair of the parent generation to cling to ownership control. If there are siblings involved who are not active in the business, the successor would like further clarity on ownership distribution. In this phase, ownership is predominantly seen as a vehicle to exercise control over the business: either maintaining it by the senior generation, or gaining control by the successor generation.

Management

The "lead to do" phase typically indicates that the successor has achieved a more viable alignment between personal aspirations, professional competence and the business needs. A certain track record leads to a higher confidence and recognition level for the successor from all stakeholders, that is family, management and employees. At this stage, the challenges shift to establishing boundaries between the influence of the outgoing and the incoming leader. Both the successor and management are confronted with an often unclear situation especially when the newly gained leadership functions of the successor are interfered with by the senior generation.

In the "lead to do" phase the successor builds up a power base and attempts to replace the existing management with a new team; one that is loyal to the successor. This is a challenging time, particularly for the business, as it becomes the potential battleground where the successor's challenges are fought out between the generations.

Individual

The "lead to do" phase is distinct from the "do" phase for the individual. The learning period allows for a period of stabilization and consolidation. The horizon shifts to medium term as the vision for the business is clearer, but the lack of ownership control is perceived as a disturbing element. At this point, the successor can focus on the growth of the business. Personal and professional recognition are a primary objective. Status plays an important role.

The successor's mindset in the "lead to do" phase now broadens to recognize the others' needs. This finds its expression in the business as the vision shifts to team-based management. The individual challenge now is to develop **organizational** leadership. At the family level, the mindset increasingly includes the needs of the new family, primarily the spouse and children.

Therefore the successor's challenges per interest level in the "lead to do" phase can be summarized as shown in Table 3.2.

Table 3.2 The successor's challenges by interest level in the "lead to do" phase

Phase / Interests	Family	Ownership	Management	Individual
Lead to do	Adult–adult relationship	Control struggle	Professional assertion	Organizational leadership

The "let do" phase

This phase typically commences around the age of 50–65. The successor's parent generation may still be alive and possibly still have some moral influence on the family business. The "let do" phase mirrors the other side of the "do" phase.

Family

The successor reaches the age where his or her children now represent the potential next generation successors. The important challenge in this phase is the construction of a positive, intergenerational relationship that integrates the experiences – both negative and positive – from the leader's own earlier succession process. The insights gained from studies conducted at IMD are that the intergenerational attachments frequently tend to shift fundamentally following a negative experience. Thus, if the successor generation had suffered from strong parental attachment, they tend to favour a detachment attitude with their own children. The reverse applies as well.

Ownership

In the "let do" phase, ownership takes a different meaning now that ownership control has finally been achieved. On the negative side, clinging to ownership is perceived as a guarantee of power and control over the next generation. On the positive side, ownership may be mentally disconnected from individual family members and be perceived as a vehicle to create wealth for a growing family and possibly over generations. From this perspective, ownership is depersonalized and institutionalized in order to provide benefits for many generations to come. The challenge, particularly in the "let do" phase, is to implement this vision through abandoning the personal power base provided by ownership control.

Management

The main challenge at this phase is the struggle with decreasing operational influence. The next generation in turn assumes leadership control, and the business typically requires adaptation and innovation. Again, this phase mirrors the challenges of the "do" phase. The loss of operational influence tends to be compensated by a stronger influence on governance levels, that is, the board of directors.

Individual

The "let do" phase also brings fundamental challenges and changes to the successor, who is now mirrored with the next successor's challenges. The main challenge on the individual level is to define a new meaning to life, distinct from the hitherto identification of self through the leadership activities in the business. This is an immensely difficult challenge that requires humility and the adoption of a long-term horizon which includes the generations to follow. The motivational needs shift from solely addressing self-esteem to self-actualization. In other words, the life achievement objective is now being defined less by their own achievements and, to a greater degree, by creating opportunities for others. The personal mindset shifts increasingly to the present and future needs of others. The individual challenge now lies in developing **institutional** leadership.

Therefore in the "let do" phase the challenges of the successor on the different interest levels can be summarized as shown in Table 3.3.

Table 3.3 The successor's challenges by interest level in the "let do phase"

Phase \ Interests	Family	Ownership	Management	Individual
Let do	Parent–child relationship	Control versus vision	Leadership assertion	Institutional leadership

The leadership phases matrix

The generational leadership challenges over the three phases of the leadership lifecycle and divided into the four interest levels can be summarized in a matrix combining the matrices from the previous section, as shown in Table 3.4 (Schwass, 2005).

Table 3.4 The leadership phases matrix

Phase \ Interests	Family	Ownership	Management	Individual
Do	Child–parent relationship	Control dependent	Professional assertion	Personal leadership
Lead to do	Adult–adult relationship	Control struggle	Leadership assertion	Organizational leadership
Let do	Parent–child relationship	Control versus vision	Governance assertion	Institutional leadership

Implications

The summarizing matrix highlights the complex challenges a next-generation leader faces in each phase, as well as the fundamental modification the challenges undergo as they shift into a different phase. It provides an analytical tool for all stakeholders to better understand each other's challenges and to prepare and plan for the needs of the next phase.

The vast majority of family businesses experience an ineffective approach by next-generation successors to leadership. Three key lessons are:

1. **Next generation leaders apply the wrong sequence**
   Upon entering the family businesses, they tend to benchmark immediately on the "lead to do" phase, omitting the learning and development experience of the "do" phase.

2. **Next generation leaders focus too narrowly**
   They attempt to gain both professional and personal assertion by focusing rapidly on leadership assertion within the management interest level – following the widely held public corporation model. By omitting to recognize and effectively address the needs of family and ownership, the successors focus excessively on their own needs to the detriment of the other stakeholders.

3. **Next generation leaders lack empathy**
   Because they tend to apply the wrong sequence in a phased leadership development process, and they focus too narrowly on the management needs instead of addressing the needs of all system stakeholders, next-generation leaders tend to be too egocentric. They are lacking empathy for other stakeholders of the family business system who have legitimate interests and needs.

The leadership phases model provides the opportunity for the next-generation leader to systematically and anticipatorily understand and plan for the most effective way of addressing the challenges. This includes the need to appreciate the benefits of sequencing through the phases and to avoid focusing on one isolated area. A final benefit is to appreciate that ultimately each successor will, in turn, face their own successor and thus mirror their own succession challenges. This should help encourage an early adoption of a more empathetic-based mindset, which is a necessary requirement for an effective family business leadership development strategy.

While the leadership phases model outlines the context for the next-generation leader, it also leads to the question of how best to orchestrate the alignment of the different needs of the four constituents: family, ownership, management and the individual. Furthermore, this alignment has to remain effective over time. What is the best way to support the creation and sustainability of an alignment?

The award-winning companies provide good examples for family businesses which have successfully aligned the four different stakeholders. They have clear objectives for each interest level that can be summarized as shown in Table 3.5 (Schwass, 2005).

Table 3.5 Stakeholders' interest by objective

Stakeholders' interest levels	Objectives
Family	Harmony by providing personal growth opportunities to all
Ownership	Wealth preservation and growth
Management	Business growth
Individual	Sense of purpose through personal growth

Growth stands out as the unifying concept which constructively addresses the needs of all interest levels over time. Ownership and management of successful family businesses directly benefit from growth strategies. Family harmony can be achieved if business growth provides more financial resources and working opportunities – if so desired – for a growing family. The growing family business provides increasing opportunities for family members to find a sense of purpose by taking an interest in community and philanthropic activities. For the individual, personal growth provides a meaningful sense of purpose in life.

The analysis into the success factors of the award-winning family businesses highlights the overall importance of growth. The outward signs of business growth are easily recognizable. Deeper underneath are other signs of growth, both on individual, personal and also process levels. The complexity of the four interest levels requires a special kind of growth, which has the capacity to effectively address multiple-level needs over time.

4
The "Wise Growth" Strategy

As shown in the preceding chapter, most successors attempt to achieve recognition as fast as possible, and they focus on business strategies before having transitioned through a development process as described earlier. The best practices learned from the award-winning family businesses highlight that business growth should be wisely constructed on the achievements, values and traditions of previous generations. Growth should not be undertaken at any cost. Evolutionary "wise growth" is more effective for family businesses than revolutionary growth. This is particularly true for those that are mindful of their traditions.

Research indicates that the evolutionary growth achieved by the award-winning companies did, indeed, very successfully link tradition with innovation. Their business growth was the result of a multilevel development process that broadly built on the concept of growth. Leaders were able to effectively manage the business growth, because they achieved a recognized leadership competence based on a leadership development process. The aspiring leader had indicated a willingness to undergo a career development process, growing the role in the business over time. Furthermore, at the beginning of this development process was the willingness to grow as an individual. The fundamental insight to take away from the award winners is that business growth is like the "tip of the iceberg"; underneath, there is a phased leadership development process which builds on the individual leader's mindset to start first with personal growth.

This insight led me to develop the concept of a three-step "wise growth" strategy. This is a strategy for family businesses to use when working out the next-generation leader's comprehensive leadership development approach:

1. **Grow as an individual**
2. **Grow your role in the business**
3. **Grow the business.**

The sequence of this growth strategy is important. A leader who is supported and respected for having systematically climbed the career ladder in the business can achieve business growth more successfully. A person who has demonstrated on an ongoing basis the desire and capacity to learn and to grow as an individual, can in turn better achieve this.

Addressing the needs of all four interest levels, over time, through a forward-oriented growth momentum is a wise strategy. The concept of "wise growth" as synthesized from the practices of the award-winning family businesses embodies this evolutionary development strategy.

Wise growth: growing as an individual

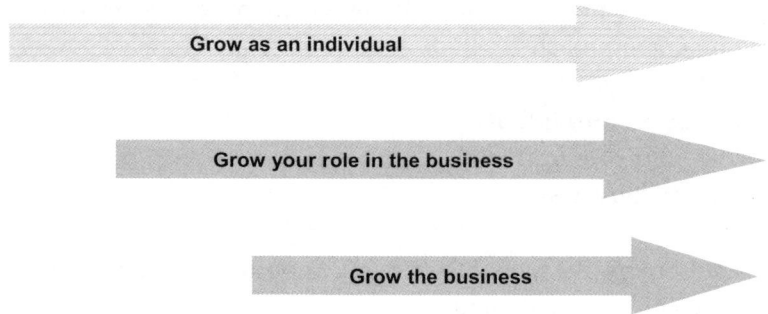

Figure 4.1   Wise growth strategy

The first dimension of the leadership development strategy is the explicit intention of the aspiring successor to take personal responsibility to grow as a person. The importance of individual growth is probably best demonstrated by the following statement made by Pietro Barilla, third-generation chairman of the Italian Barilla Group, as he was about to retire: "As family members leading a family business, we must offer something of ourselves – the best of what we are." Jean-Louis Dumas, fifth-generation leader at Hermès, echoed this: "The secret of our company lies in a job well done – everyone should be proud of doing his or her best."

My research into the success factors of the award-winning family businesses highlights that leaders are driven by the desire to continuously discover new and better ways to manage the business. This ongoing process of adaptation to the changing environment and changing needs is, in fact, the extension of the desire – or the need – to grow as an individual. The strategy of growing as an individual ties in with the "do" and "lead to do" phases that were described in the leadership phases development process in Chapter 3. The capacity to grow as an individual is most obvious when the company is founded: by definition, the entrepreneur thrives on being different and disruptive to established norms. Building a successful business in the first generation requires mental strength and growth.

All of the award-winning family businesses include examples of the subsequent generations clearly displaying signs of a deep commitment to ongoing individual growth. Pushing to discover and overcome one's own limitations through lifelong learning builds on a degree of humility that is a key requirement for leadership in a family business. Humility encourages family and ownership support, and it reinforces the view that the family business is a multigenerational institution. Individual growth happens on two dimensions. Firstly, to better oneself: the objective here is to never actually achieve an absolute target, but rather to continuously identify new areas of learning and improvement. The second dimension is the desire to discover the best possible learning path. The following paragraph highlights best practices from the award winners.

Who wants to grow?

In the beginning, each aspiring successor in the family business needs to internalize the commitment and willingness to develop and grow as an individual in order to be respected by others, both family and non-family. A large part of this respect is already earned, in fact, simply by the successors' willingness to submit to a process of personal development through learning. Therefore, it is important that the successor proactively starts this initiative, rather than responding to pressure from the parent generation. With respect to the individual development dimension, there appear to be two types of successors. The first type possesses an inherent character trait, typically based on a sense of curiosity, which naturally pushes the successor in their desire to grow. The second type needs to develop this willingness to grow. Research on successor development in family businesses indicates that this is best triggered through the inspiration of successful leaders. While the inspirational leaders can be from other businesses and fields, many successors, in fact, appear to be often deeply inspired by the founders, or other earlier-generation leaders of the family business. For example, the fourth-generation successor team in the Italian Zegna Group openly express their admiration for the leaders from the previous generations, and most particularly for Ermenegildo Zegna who, in the second generation, laid the foundation for the strong growth of the family business. The important message to take away is that this willingness for personal development can be acquired.

The willingness to grow, as an individual, needs to be guided by objectives. For a successor aspiring to a leadership role, the individual growth objectives can typically be taken from leadership qualifications displayed by successful leaders. As mentioned earlier, these can be individuals from inside or outside the family business who serve as an inspiration to the successor and thereby trigger the very willingness to grow. What qualities do leaders possess that can serve as a guideline towards achieving personal growth? Interviews with senior and well-experienced leaders – often retired – of leading family businesses produced the following list (Schwass, 2005):

Qualities needed for effective leadership

- Knowledgeable
- Experienced
- Logical
- Decisive
- Courageous
- Devoted
- Creative
- Intuitive
- Energetic
- Engaging
- Optimistic

The qualities of knowledge and experience are necessary for all leaders. A successor's growth is necessarily built upon their acquisition of knowledge and experience. But not all leaders necessarily have all of the listed qualities, and there are some leaders who have other qualities. The point is that successors need to be attracted and inspired by at least one or several of these leadership qualities in others. Typically, this is a highly individual process which varies from person to person.

How can a potential successor most effectively grow as an individual by acquiring knowledge and experience? Again, this varies from person to person. But both research into successful family businesses and modern learning theories indicate that a well-structured learning process greatly enhances the acquisition of knowledge and experience for a family business successor. The evolution of learning theories can be described as follows. In the past, learning was seen as an informational process which consisted of acquiring and storing knowledge. In this context, knowledge is seen as rational. In the 1980s, new research emerged which challenged this assumption. Learning was seen as a transformational process that modifies the learner's general worldview and basic assumptions. The human being is not just seen as a machine that stores rational information; instead, emotions are acknowledged and learning is greatly enhanced by linking experience and emotions (Hill, 2001). Kolb introduced four steps in this transformational learning process; these steps are summarized below (Kolb, 1984).

Kolb's learning model

- Concrete experience – this fully involves the person
- Reflective observation – provides relevant information and different perspectives
- Abstract conceptualization – leads to an analytical model
- Active experimentation – allows structured and systematic testing.

Firstly, concrete experience fully involves the person. Secondly, reflective observation provides all relevant information regarding this experience and from different perspectives. Thirdly, abstract conceptualization leads to an analytical model which categorizes experience into logically sound theories. Fourthly, active experimentation allows for a structured and systematic testing of new concepts in new situations by using these theories to make decisions and solve problems. Kolb noticed that learning often begins with a concrete experience.

The importance of experience

This model is particularly relevant for the potential successor who wants to grow as a person, because it stresses the importance of experience in the learning cycle. In this learning model, it is better to have a large number of varied experiences. If these are then appropriately analysed and conceptualized, they can lead to better knowledge, which in turn leads to stronger transformational capabilities. But research into typical family business successor development highlights that the most common practice appears to be limiting the successors' experience to the family business. By doing so, the abstract conceptualization step is limited to a much narrower view – the successors' family business. In addition, active experimentation inside the family business is not easy for a young potential successor; their lack of competence and their connection to the owning family are eyed critically by all stakeholders. Therefore, active experimentation may not even be possible for the young successor, or it may only be possible under very difficult circumstances. This develops into a somewhat vicious circle: limited experience leads to limited understanding and conceptualization with limited application possibilities in the family business. Recent research into the typical characteristics of bad leaders highlights insularity as one reason for failing leadership (Kellerman, 2004). Best practices from successful family businesses point towards a three-phased approach which can more effectively enhance the successor's individual growth.

Phase one. This is essentially limited to developing as an individual within the context of the family business. While this makes it difficult for the successor to apply any early active experimentation, the benefit is that a deep understanding of the family business is developed. Phase one usually starts in the early to mid-teens and often reaches into the final stages of an academic education. Note that this starts even before the "do" phase in the leadership development phases framework. Concrete experience is gained through early short and part-time activities, such as summer jobs. Certain families, however, prefer their young next-generation members not to be exposed to the business during the formative years for fear of failure. In this case, the next generation can learn and experience new things by going on field trips, either accompanied by senior family members or as a group of siblings and cousins demonstrating an interest and curiosity in the business. Visiting subsidiaries in foreign countries can be a most stimulating and intellectually rewarding experience. The next-generation members of the Henkel family regularly meet within the "information circle" and arrange study tours to foreign factories within the Henkel Group. The respect shown by local employees in appreciation of this interest shown by the ownership in the business is often an enlightening experience for younger next-generation members who may question their own value added to the business.

In this phase, the most meaningful learning comes from interactions with senior-generation family members. It is striking that many multigenerational family businesses create both formal and informal opportunities for intergenerational learning. This can take place during family reunions and celebrations where time is provided for the young generation to ask questions. In some cases, the next-generation potential successors interview older-generation family members about their experiences and write an article or book where the family's history and values are captured. Understanding the history of the family business through the eyes of senior-generation family members is, in fact, one of the most valuable initiatives a successor can undertake. These are extremely important opportunities to transmit the family mission from one generation to the next. Interviews with current and former employees and other stakeholders – suppliers, clients, bankers – also provide valuable outside perspectives. Many of the family members interviewed attested to the strong motivational and inspirational effect of meeting with very senior employees and workers – often retired – who remembered the former-generation family members. These encounters tend to bring out stories of particular events and significance which are transmitted from generation to generation. The Johnson, Barilla and Zegna families are particularly explicit examples of young generations who have found ways to meaningfully benefit – and internalize – from the experience and wisdom of their parent generations. This is of particular relevance also for the later determination of wise business growth strategies. The most successful multigenerational family businesses are very effective at strategically linking their traditions with innovations. When the successor generations introduce innovative business strategies, they can "wisely" use past practices and strategies. Therefore, the successor's deep understanding of the family business' history is absolutely essential.

Many of the researched award-winning family businesses explicitly stated their mission to improve the quality of life of their clients and the communities where they are active. The way to achieve this is by making products and offering services which truly make a difference. The Johnson family's focus on "product plus" is one example of this attitude. Product plus is the concept that every new Johnson product had to have a distinct advantage over everything else on the market, or it had to be new and unique enough to outstrip the competition. In conversations with today's next-generation family members, this mission to make a difference strongly resonated. Another determining factor for the level of interest in the family business is the type of corporate citizenship exercised by the family and the business. Each of the award winners gives back generously to the community and to various causes – and they are selected for the award partly because of this characteristic. Some do so visibly with a high degree of professionalism and transparency. This is the case of the Samuel C. Johnson Family Enterprises which publishes an annual report of its broad range of philanthropic activities. The Kristiansen family of LEGO contributed to the airport at Billund where their head office is located. It is now the second largest airport in Denmark. Many families donate substantial sums to their communities for educational and cultural causes (Bonnier) and for hospitals (Barilla). The visible and measurable concern that these family business owners have for the environment and the community is a powerful motivational influence especially to the younger, next-generation members.

Another highly effective form of learning is for several generations of the family to jointly attend a family business seminar. One private programme conducted at IMD was initiated by a third-generation successor who wanted to learn as much as possible about the history of the family business. The participants came from three generations. The outcome was that all generations agreed to continue to run the business as a family business, because the successor's desire and commitment to prepare for the leadership role visibly grew over the course of the programme.

Essentially, in phase one, the potentially strongest individual growth opportunities are based on learning from others connected to the family business, particularly senior family members. The small and intimate group size of this type of interaction lends itself ideally to meaningful discussions based on reflective observations and abstract conceptualizations. Structured learning events can then potentially increase the depth and breadth of the learning. The award-winning family businesses are, without exception, examples of having a focused commitment to studies: while the first and founding generations typically were lacking formal education, they ensured that their children benefited from the best available educational resources. The most striking example is second-generation Ermenegildo Zegna: his education was entrusted to the local parish priest at the age of six, thereby creating the base for his social vision of an entrepreneur's role. From early on, language studies were seen as a vehicle to be able to expand the learning and experiences to other countries. The Zegna family is also a good example of how succeeding generations continue to emphasize education. The third and fourth generations, from very young ages, were brought up with nannies that spoke different languages. Higher academic studies, in disciplines directly related to the family business, are common, increasingly so, at highly reputed schools. The families that own LEGO, Puig and Zegna are all strong examples of this practice. In family businesses where the next-generation leadership is intended to be shared by a team of two or more, it is common for the interested leaders to specialize – both educationally and functionally. The most typical splitting into disciplines is business administration and technical studies. But other specializations can also occur. For example, after the unexpected death of one second-generation son in the Murugappa family, the other two second-generation sons split their roles into "Mr Inside" and "Mr Outside". Another example is in the Bonnier family where the fifth-generation members distributed management responsibilities according to their different markets (newspapers, magazines and publishing).

Phase two. The learning process now shifts away from the family business and the family. Through concrete work and life experiences in new and different environments, the individual's capacity for abstract conceptualization is greatly enriched. The next-generation leader's family and family business are no longer the only focus. Therefore, new, meaningful benchmarking can take place. Professional work experiences in other businesses or industries also provide active experimentation opportunities; opportunities that were much more difficult to find in their own family business. Therefore, the learning cycle in phase two is greatly enhanced compared to phase one. In many of the award-winning family businesses, the successor viewed outside experience as an opportunity to escape from overpowering senior-generation family leaders and, thereby, develop a greater sense of independence. Guido Barilla, fourth-generation chairman of the Barilla Group from Italy, indicated that he moved to New York in his early years in order to be independent from his father. Very similarly, fourth-generation Gildo Zegna, from the Italian Zegna Group, started his working career as a buyer at Bloomingdale's in New York.

For many of the leading family businesses, this outside experience is seen as a major career development step. In some cases, the potential successors are required to show at least two important promotions before being admitted as a leadership candidate in the family business. Others require the next generation to make their own arrangements for outside experience, including finding employment. They believe that by not providing assistance, the next generation is exposed to a valuable decision-making process that helps grow their sense of independence.

Research shows that there are two distinct objectives in obtaining this outside experience. Firstly, it provides an opportunity to gain a better understanding of the same industry that the family business is in, in order to return with new and different knowledge that will be helpful later on in growing the business. The second objective is to develop a sense of independence and competence as a business person. The insight from the award-winning family businesses is that, on average, the first objective appears to prevail. It is the one that is made explicit, and the senior generation typically expresses a preference for an outside activity in a related business. Interviews with next-generation family leaders have brought out some different views: their perspective appears to be related to more independence. This independence can be more easily achieved in an industry and a business where the family connection is not known. Consider fourth-generation Paolo Barilla's motor racing career and his move to work for Toyota in Japan before joining the family business at the age of 30. This experience had to provide him insight into Toyota's quality processes that could then be applied to their industry. In fact, members of well-known families often experience difficulties in finding meaningful outside working opportunities, because the potential employer assumes that any job will only be temporary. There are examples, however, where both objectives could have been effectively achieved. At Hermès, fifth-generation leader Jean-Louis Dumas worked as a buyer for competitors. This outside experience was seen as highly valuable for the business turnaround he engineered in the 1980s.

Phase three. The learning process now takes place within the family business as the successor begins a leadership career. It is now increasingly possible to experience the full learning cycle – including active experimentation – since the successor comes back to the family business with a knowledge and experience base that has been greatly enhanced by time "outside". This strengthens both the successor's self-confidence, and the recognition and respect that others now have for the leader. In many cases, the formal entry into the family business starts at a subsidiary level: it serves as a safety net for the leader before they are confronted with the central activities of the family business. Later on, when preparing for a governance role, a seat on a subsidiary's board provides similar learning opportunities before full exposure to the overall board. The individual growth process continues: many successors who saw benefits to being distanced from the family and the family business during phase two, actively search for continuing learning and development opportunities outside the family and its business when they return to their roots. Associations such as the Young Presidents' Organization and the Family Business Network provide opportunities to meet with peers from other family businesses in different industries and regions. This enables personal benchmarking which can stimulate the desire for ongoing individual growth. These and other organizations, such as business schools, offer focused educational programmes and learning activities addressing different needs. Growing as an individual ideally becomes a mindset over time, where growing through learning is never really completed. Another way to grow is to take a sabbatical. The third-generation leader of LEGO did so and came back with a new management framework. The Johnson family provides another example of this kind of intellectual distancing and renewal. In 1935, the third-generation leader took time off to lead a 22,000-mile expedition from Milwaukee to the Brazilian rain forest. He returned invigorated and full of new visions for the business. In 1998, his son and two grandsons replicated the trip. They also returned invigorated.

To summarize, the first requirement for growing as an individual is the willingness to grow. This can be acquired, typically through inspiration by respected leaders, family members or traditions. The most meaningful inspiration and learning can come from a deep and broad understanding of the family business history. Some families, like the Murugappas, specifically direct senior-generation leaders to mentor next-generation members thus providing full support in an institutionalized way. The vehicle applied to individual growth is an iterative process of learning and experiencing. Structuring this process in three phases – inside the family business, then outside and finally inside again – provides growth opportunities which are of particular relevance to family business successors. This reduces the risk of insularity and lack of professional and personal benchmarking.

Ongoing contacts with peers serve as valuable personal benchmarking mechanisms underpinning the motivation for continuous growth.

Growing as an individual: Risks and opportunities

Risk A. A key risk in the individual growth dimension originates from the senior generation of family members. As the next-generation leader attempts to create a growing number of learning and experience opportunities, first inside and then outside the family business, the senior generation needs to respect their apparent growing distance and the need to learn from others and in different ways. This is particularly relevant in regard to their role as teachers for the next generation. Research into learning has identified four stages in the evolution of learning needs and their respective support structure (Grow, 1988: 137).

1. Dependent student – authority
2. Interested student – motivator
3. Involved student – facilitator
4. Self-directed student – consultant.

This model highlights the evolution in one's learning needs over time. The senior generation must be aware that the typical learning process requires a decreasing role of authority-based teaching until the final stage, when the self-directed learner freely selects the teacher or the support who can best address their needs at that time. Not understanding this evolution may put the senior generation in an authoritarian teaching mode that keeps the student dependent. In many family businesses this happens intentionally. The senior generation want to maintain their authority over the next generation in order not to lose control over the business and the family. Another risk originates from other members of the same generation – siblings or cousins – who do not subscribe to the same level of willingness to grow as an individual. The commitment to learn and experience may be perceived with suspicion, and jealousy and rivalry may break out.

Opportunity A. These risks can be perceived as opportunities for a greater, joint learning experience that has some benefits for all. This appears to work best when the next-generation member adopts a "pull" attitude by formally and informally inviting others to join in. The learning becomes a transparent process which ultimately can benefit the entire family. The key, again, is the humility displayed by the next-generation member.

Risk B. Another important risk in the individual growth dimension is the possibility that the next-generation member – often during the course of the outside experience – does not wish to return to the family business. The outside career opportunities may be more attractive than those inside the family business.

Opportunity B. A vehicle used by many of the leading family businesses to address this risk is the ongoing involvement of the next generation in some type of formal activity. With regard to the business, this may be on a special forward-oriented development committee which helps retain the interest and motivation to return. Strategic experiments regarding new products, processes, markets and distribution channels can provide an exciting perspective, even with minimal time involvement. On the family side, participating in family council committees which work on forward-oriented development projects, that is, education and philanthropy, may also retain an interest and excitement for the family business.

Wise Growth: growing the role in the business

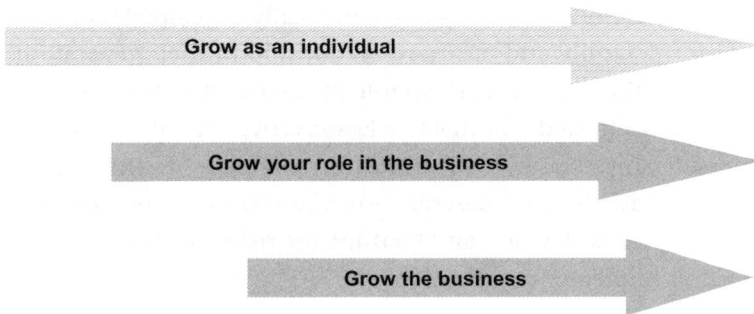

Figure 4.1 Wise growth strategy

Growing your role in the business is the second component of the "wise growth" strategy, and follows the initial willingness to grow as an individual. The insights from the award winners clearly point to a general evolution over time on how the next generation becomes interested in the business. Without doubt, in the early generations of the researched businesses, there simply was no choice – the next generation was expected and had to join the family business. The clearest examples are Henkel and Puig where the founder told the children to stay united in the family business. In the case of the Puig family, the gravity of this message was reinforced because it was the last wish of the founder and expressed on his death bed. When it was not verbalized, the expectations by the parent generation that the next generation would stay and lead the business seemed to be omnipresent! The business horizon of the early generations tended to be longer and stretched into the next generations. A visible sign of this mindset was the residential proximity: the next generation lived in the same house or very close by. It is only in the later and current generations that the issue of free choice has surfaced. Today, the focus is shifting increasingly to understanding the motivational power of free choice and setting out an effective and transparent career development process. The research insights from the award-winning family businesses suggest that a structured and manageable process is the best approach. There are three important lessons. Firstly, the family involved outside advice in regard to career planning. Secondly, the next-generation owners have systematically developed their own vision for the family and business relationship in their generation. Thirdly, over time, the leadership role in the business was critically evaluated and adjusted. The first two lessons cover the "do" and "lead to do" leadership phases, while the last lesson relates to the "let do" leadership phase. Below, I describe how the award-winning families implemented these lessons, and I outline the risks and opportunities involved in implementing them.

Independent outside advice

A second-generation successor who started to work in his family business expressed his experience about growing his role in the business as follows: "When I entered the business, I experienced a whole new world. When the business was successful, it was credited to how well the previous generation had planned everything for me. When the business was not successful, I took all the blame."

The previous chapter described the complex issues a successor entering the business faces. They were summarized as follows:

- A business culture defined by one individual
- A business strategy adapted to the experiences of the outgoing leader
- A given parent–child relationship between the outgoing and the incoming leader, in the most common succession cases.

The potential for conflict is high, particularly during transitions, due to issues that link the family and the business, which in turn mixes rationality and emotionality. There is solid evidence from the award-winning family businesses that they have benefited from different types of qualified outside advice. This is particularly true for the leadership transitions which took place within the last four to five decades. As I show below, the nature of the advice can be categorized into two categories – functionally specific advice and broader interdisciplinary advice, which facilitates intergenerational communication.

Functionally specific advice in this context typically refers to human resources-based career planning support, as shown in the following case. When fourth-generation Sam Johnson entered his family business, Samuel C. Johnson & Sons in the US, his father, HF, on the advice of a consulting firm (Booz, Allen and Hamilton), developed a career plan for Sam. Against his initial resistance, Sam was taken through several internal learning assignments before being given the task of running the newly created "new product development" department. Later on in life, Sam affirmed the wisdom and benefits of this professional development process. It helped build trust and confidence from people around the young successor. In addition, the recommendation to work in a newly created department with the objective to develop new products was laudable since it minimized – at least initially – competition with existing structures.

Broader interdisciplinary advice links family and business needs and, through a holistic assessment, develops approaches that are of benefit not only for one individual but for the entire family business. The Henkel Group and the Puig Group have made extensive and continued use of interdisciplinary outside advice during the last two generations, supporting the next-generation leaders' growing role in the business. The fundamental benefit of this type of advice is that qualified outsiders can separate the emotions from the issues. They can assess family business issues more easily in terms of structural and system needs rather than personality-driven issues. Besides knowledge, they also bring perspective. The Zegna Group provides another relevant example. An outside consultant who was already working with the third generation and understood the needs of the business as well as the family advised the fourth-generation successors, Paolo and Gildo. The added benefit was a less emotional intergenerational relationship, as well as neutral and rational career advice. The rationalization and professionalism added by outsiders are especially valuable for managing intergenerational relationships. Jealousies and competition between siblings and cousins can be more effectively addressed and resolved if there is a well-structured, transparent and outside-guided development process.

Ideally, potential successors who decide to work in the family business should follow a professional career development plan. This provides an independent, professional assessment of the strengths and weaknesses of the successor's skills and leads to a progress plan based on performance milestones. This eliminates the usual criticisms – both from family and non-family members – which young successors are often confronted with, namely that they have been appointed because of who they are rather than what they are. A professional career plan is particularly important when the successor is young and has little outside experience. As mentioned earlier, the leader would have worked, ideally, for several years outside, independent from the family business, and this experience would have helped shape both personal and business understanding. It would also provide a higher degree of self-confidence, and the security of knowing their market value. The advice of qualified advisors throughout the entire career is of fundamental value in effectively developing the necessary leadership skills.

Independent outside advice: risks and opportunities

Risk A. The biggest risk of involving an outsider as a career advisor to the next generation is that the senior generation uses that advisor to transmit and reinforce their own vision for the future and the implied role of the next generation. Thus the advisor runs the risk of appearing as an extended voice of the senior generation. This is a real risk, because in most cases the advisor is not paid by the next generation and is even selected by the outgoing generation.

Opportunity A. A potential opportunity is that the outside advisor may grow into a mentoring role. This can be achieved through a clearly and transparently defined assignment for the outsider; ideally, both generations would be involved from an early stage in defining the boundaries. Certain elements should remain confidential between the advisor and the next-generation family member. The advisor may thus provide continuing support in a mentoring spirit.

Risk B. There is the risk – and often the temptation – to draw on the business' internal human resource department to draw up the career plan for the next generation. While they do understand the needs of the business and often have an outside understanding of the family needs, it creates conflicts of interest for employees when they are asked to plan career aspects for their future superior.

Opportunity B. The opportunity here is that the human resources department would develop a meaningful relationship with the next generation family leader and the business management. Many HR employees see the "moment of truth" when they feel that they have to declare their loyalty to the outgoing generation, particularly if they have worked in parallel over an extended time period. Management is best advised to adopt an attitude of being loyal to the business rather than being loyal to a person. Furthermore, expressing the difficulties such an in-house assignment might bring to them creates a new platform of open communication with both generations.

The visioning process

The other key element in growing one's role in the business is the "visioning" process. Each business starts with a vision. The most common entrepreneurial vision is based on the founding entrepreneur's need for personal independence. In some cases the business vision is product or service based from the beginning. More often the vision emerges after a period of experimentation and adaptation, which may take years. Any long-term successful business needs to have a vision which rallies a group of people around an achievable idea. In the founding generation, the vision is typically closely identified with the person who started the business. It is hugely gratifying for an entrepreneur to be identified with a successful vision. Although the temptation is great to impress onto the next generation the benefits and success of the vision and to make the succeeding generation adopt it as their own, analysis into multigenerational success factors clearly indicates that family businesses benefit greatly when each generation defines its own vision. Process is more important than content: the next generation may indeed share the predecessor's vision but they need to arrive at this conclusion by following their own independent visioning process. It is only after such a process that they can truly experience a sense of ownership in the adopted vision. Thus the visioning process has an energizing quality. In addition, effective leadership is built on a vision that can credibly be transmitted throughout the organization. The effectiveness of the leader is undoubtedly higher if everyone inside and outside the business can identify the vision with the current leader.

Ideally, with the encouragement of the outgoing generation, the successor generation develops and formulates their vision for the family business. This is a formal process that obliges the successor to examine sustainable roles for each individual – both in the family and the business – during their tenure. The key question to answer is: "What roles will the family play, both as owners and as managers, in the business throughout this new generation?" Since the vision eventually defines the future they hope for at the highest possible conceptual level, all members of the next generation are typically involved. Outside consultants usually help conduct this process, because it requires an educational introduction and a professionally supervised execution. During the educational introduction, the next-generation members (typically at least 18 years old) are exposed to the current theories on family businesses as well as family business cases that are both similar and different to their family business. In the next step, they are given individual assignments where they have to imagine and compose an article for a leading business magazine that describes their family business in 10–15 years' time. This forward projection requires them to structure and verbalize their dream for the family business and, by implication, their own possible future role. Guidelines are given in support of this assignment. During the next step, the individual reports back with their completed assignment in front of the entire next-generation group. A careful analysis extracts the similarities and differences. The differences are discussed and explored with regard to their relevance for the future. Depending on their importance, follow-up activities may be required in order to appropriately address these differences. In some cases, they may lead to decisions on separation and "pruning" of the family tree. Usually, this is perceived as constructive, because it is part of an open, transparent and trusting process that facilitates the best possible solution in a manageable and peaceful spirit. Focusing on the similarities allows the next generation to craft a common and shared vision statement. Typically, these address the value-added role of the family in the business on the ownership and the management levels. The following are examples of vision statements crafted by next-generation members. They do not originate from any award-winning business, and they reflect very diverse backgrounds.

Vision statement for the family

- **Example A**

  "It is the family's desire to stay together around shared values applying the concept of a family-in-business, whereby the family adds value to the business, and the business is a means to involve family in the community.

  It is the family's desire to achieve this through a successful business, where the family is visible and which employees are proud to work for, implementing a strategy of dynamic, global, and professional growth, and developing innovative quality products."

- **Example B**

  "The family commits to work together by building trust and respect for each other's diverse identities.

  The family wants to exercise enlightened, responsible and active team ownership in sustainable businesses managed to the highest professional standards of excellence."

The vision statement is then formally submitted by the next generation to the senior generation. It is important that this is part of a formal meeting which underscores the real and true importance of this document. Once the next generation has formally submitted the outcome to the parent generation, it becomes a psychologically liberating experience. The significance resembles "cutting the umbilical cord", which symbolically marks the end of the parent–child relationship. If not explicit, by implication, the visioning statement makes allowances for the role of the outgoing generation, in an empathetic and constructive form. This further enhances the building of trust between generations and, thereby, continues to support the growing role of the next generation in the business. The Henkel Group and the Puig Group have both successfully applied the visioning process for the current generations.

The visioning process: risks and opportunities

Risk A. The most common risk is that the visioning process does not obtain full support from family members. The outgoing generation may wish the next generation to adhere to the past vision and may not want to open the door to any possible dissent. The next generation may feel inadequate and possibly too immature to conduct this process.

Opportunity A. The opportunity, through this visioning process, is to provide the next generation with a development and expression platform that optimizes the outcome. Sooner or later, the next generation has to reflect on their future role in their family. By formalizing and structuring this as a process, valuable time and opportunity costs may be avoided as the most important outcome is clarity in their future objectives. And, by professionalizing the process, the chances for a higher quality and more meaningful outcome are greater. The senior generation often better understands the full value and benefits of a visioning process by learning from families who have actually completed it.

Risk B. A very real risk is that the next generation undertakes this process and submits a vision statement that is not received or recognized by the senior generation. Unexplained rejection by the senior generation will enforce conflicts.

Opportunity B. In this case, the senior generation needs to analyse the underlying reasons for its rejection and enter into a joint discussion and reflection process with the next generation. Qualified outside facilitators can direct this interaction towards a meaningful learning and consensus building experience for both generations. In this context, process tends to become more important than content. A valuable intergenerational discussion process will eventually lead to a solution.

Evolving the leadership role

The award-winning family businesses provide many meaningful examples for how family leadership was developed and how it evolved. As shown in the previous chapter, the leadership lifecycle has three phases: "do", "lead to do" and "let do". The corresponding phased interests, as experienced by the next-generation leader, are: personal leadership, organizational leadership and lastly institutional leadership. The most valuable commonality found in the family businesses researched in this context is the capacity to understand the role of leadership in a dynamic, evolving context. Growing a family member's leadership role in the business is subjected to a transparent process which is more harmonious, the higher the degree of humility of the leader. Leadership development and its evolutionary role in these family businesses were not discussed behind closed doors. In most cases, this was the result of a constructive process that was triggered by an internal or external event. The career development plan for the third-generation Johnson leader, discussed earlier, is one such example.

One interesting dimension of this process is to view leadership succession as an event that deserves to be celebrated. Passing the baton from one generation to the next is an important milestone not only for those who are directly concerned, but equally for stakeholders from inside and outside the business who may wonder and also speculate about future changes. Leadership transitions create uncertainties and emotional turmoil for those whose role changes. When the leadership succession took place between the second and third generation of the Puig Corporation in Spain, it was formally staged as a celebration. Over 120 key managers, clients, suppliers and others – even the corporate tax inspector – were invited to join the family in celebrating this event. The outgoing generation gave a presentation of historic milestones. Thereafter, the successor generation presented their plans for the future strategy. The formality of this event clarified the beginning of a new leadership era to all stakeholders. The achievements of the outgoing generation were appropriately recognized and celebrated. And the successor generation were assured of broadly based support for their vision for the family business. The formality of the event provided transparent clarity on the roles of different family members and it celebrated the growth of the next-generation leaders in the business.

As the next generation exercises leadership control, events may arise where it is appropriate to question the leadership role held by one or several family members. The trigger may be internal changes in the family or business, for example the death of key senior family members or the need for new business strategies. There may also be external triggers due to political and market related changes. Sometimes these forces all come at the same time. This was the case for the Murugappa Group. In 1995, India joined the World Trade Organization, which opened up new markets and opportunities. The following year, two key family members unexpectedly passed away. This triggered the desire for an assessment of the role of family members as leaders of subsidiaries in the family-owned conglomerate. At a time of fascinating new expansion possibilities, was it really effective to have senior family members continue as management leaders of subsidiaries? Furthermore, in the long run, with subsidiaries in different industries developing at different paces, what would be the effect on family harmony? The assessment of the leadership role of family members – conducted with outside advice – came to the conclusion that the subsidiaries could also be effectively managed by competent non-family professionals, thus freeing family members to contribute to the growth of the group in new and better ways. The vision for the business evolved from a collection of subsidiaries to that of a group which was owned by one holding company. Underneath the holding company, a new corporate board was created with both family members and independent directors. The family members now had three clearly defined responsibilities:

1. Functional responsibility across all business units
2. Oversee/mentor one or more business units (which they had never led before)
3. Mentor young family members for a future governance role.

External and internal triggers led to a process of redesigning the family leadership role in the business. One important lesson, which can be drawn from this example, is the willingness of the family leadership to submit itself to a critical assessment of its role. Underlying this is the recognition that the needs of the family as a group were greater than the needs of the individual. Shifting from the "lead to do" to a "let do" role requires the leader to adapt and grow into a new function on the governance level. On an individual level, this is often perceived as difficult since it involves a loss of direct influence. Gaining experience on different boards prior to handing over management leadership, in order to move to a governance position, is an appropriate preparation for the new form of influence. Third-generation Mariano Puig Sr, chairman of the Puig Corporation in Spain, having handed over leadership to the next generation and moved on to chair the board, said: "My role is to ensure that the right questions are being asked, but not to give answers; that, my successors should do."

Another valuable example for the implications of an evolving leadership role is the Henkel Group. When fourth-generation leader Konrad Henkel stepped down at the age of 65 as the last family leader of the business, a new structure was created for the family to retain a controlling influence. However, since the next CEO was a non-family member, the nature of the family influence on the business clearly changed: it was now ownership based. The family had clearly defined its vision: to be involved owners and to create an effective platform for influencing the business. A new shareholders committee was created with five family members and four independent outsiders. The outsiders were all highly respected and experienced senior business leaders and included the former chairman of the Nestlé group. The shareholder committee delegated the responsibility to manage the business to a management board that consisted exclusively of non-family members. The influence of the family on the business continued to be strong and accepted by the management thanks to the high quality of the decisions and value added by the shareholder committee.

The key lesson here is that a family withdrawing from management needs to be concerned about the quality and professionalism of its modified influence on the business. A weakened family influence creates a vacuum in the decision-making process that tends to be filled by management. The award-winning family businesses are examples for families who are intent on maintaining a strong strategic influence on the business and who are careful about adapting this influence following internal or external triggers. Often it takes a period of testing out various forms of formal – and informal – influences before a family settles on a structure that they feel comfortable with. Key success factors for this new form of influence are a high quality of value added, and the involvement of independent, professional outsiders. Another example of an evolving leadership influence is the Barilla Group. After the death of the third-generation leader Pietro Barilla, his four children exercised leadership interest in different forms of ownership and management positions during several years. Today, they define their role as being there to "influence the business but not interfere". Besides their role on the board of the holding company and various subsidiaries, they participate as active owners on three key committees, which focus on brand, new products and performance reviews.

To summarize, growing the next-generation leader's role in the business is most effective within the framework of a structured process. This includes involving independent outside advice, either on special functional issues or on an interdisciplinary, broader family business base. The next generation must explicitly formulate their own vision for the future of the family business. It is only then that a real sense of emotional ownership – in addition to financial ownership – will set in. Furthermore, the new vision is comforting to the outgoing generation, in terms of the generational sustainability of the family business, and it facilitates ownership transition planning. Finally, the leadership role evolves over time, either in predictable phases or unpredictably following internal or external triggers. The award-winning families share both the concern about the continuing strategic family influence in the business and the capacity to adapt and express this influence in different value-added ways, thus recreating a new equilibrium for all interest levels.

Evolving the leadership role: risks and opportunities

Risk A. The key risk is that the family does not recognize the need for leadership evolution. The triggers are not understood or perceived as not being relevant. This risk is particularly great for family businesses which are too inward focused. Often, it is simply easier to continue as before and to not upset a structure and equilibrium that has adequately functioned so far. The opportunity costs may only arise at a later stage.

Opportunity A. Since leadership evolution has first and foremost an effect – often negative – on the individual leader, the decision-making process needs to be formalized. Structures such as a working family council and a board of directors, with independent outsiders, are best placed to understand the implications following external or internal changes. In addition, they have the power to implement changes.

Risk B. The other key risk in this context is that the family addresses the leadership evolution incorrectly. The risk is great that family emotions and pressures influence the discussions and decisions around changing leadership, rather than focusing on process.

Opportunity B. Independent outside advice can make this process less emotional and create an appropriate and professional setting for the family to assess the situation. The real opportunity exists for the family to jointly explore changes as something not to be feared but rather as a platform for constructive and positive evolution. How to handle change requires a well-prepared and transparent process, which provides comfort to all stakeholders.

Wise growth: growing the business

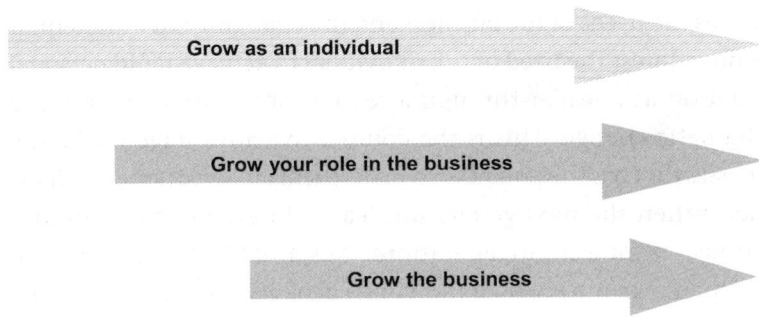

Figure 4.1 Wise growth strategy

Growing the business is the third component of the "wise growth" strategy. It follows the leader's willingness to grow as an individual and the structured approach they take towards growing their role in the business. Growing the business is the logical extension of the growth mentality that the next generation had already displayed. The first two growth components build the necessary internal mindset for the next-generation member aspiring to lead the family business. Importantly, it builds trust with the parent generation and other stakeholders. This trust creates the appropriate environment for the final area to apply the growth strategy – the business.

Business growth ideally addresses the needs of all four interest levels in the family business. A growing family benefits from the opportunities that a growing business offers. Ownership benefits through increased wealth and dividend possibilities. Management benefits from stable employment and higher compensation. Lastly, the individual, as the leader, benefits from business growth in a most important way. The need by the next-generation leaders to be seen and recognized as entrepreneurs in their own right is the most powerful motivator for business growth in the family business. Business growth is the outward sign of affirmation and independence for the next generation. But it is not just any growth which distinguishes the award-winning family businesses. Their growth strategy follows a certain logic over multiple generations: evolutionary "wise growth". The business development strategy adopted by each generation addresses the needs of the business and the changing environment; it does not address the need of the individual to achieve rapid personal affirmation as a leader through a revolutionary strategy building on dramatic change. This is the competitive advantage for family businesses that has the potential to make them an exceptional business model. When the next-generation leader internalizes a humility-based vision for a multigenerational sustainable business model, rather than maximizing their individual benefits at the expense of the family and ownership, all available resources can be put to the most effective use in the business. This is why the "wise growth" strategy components are so important. It is the demonstrated willingness to grow as an individual and as a leader which attracts the support of family and ownership to the aspiring leader, who can then devote all available resources and energy to growing the business. In addition, the early immersion into the family business culture would bring a deep understanding and appreciation of the historic achievements – and investments – of the family as owners and leaders of a business. The award-winning family businesses highlight how each generation has managed growth in a "wise" evolutionary way. Below are some common categories for business growth strategies:

Business growth strategies

- Internationalization
- Diversification to related products
- Diversification to unrelated products
- Vertical integration.

All of the award-winning family businesses, over time, applied one or several of these growth strategies. It is remarkable to note that each generation appeared to choose its own particular strategy, which was then applied during its own lifecycle. Tables 4.1–3 show how these family businesses evolved through multiple generations.

Table 4.1 Generational growth strategies: Henkel

Generation	Leader	Ownership	Business	Strategy
1	Fritz	100%	Detergent	Monoline
2	Fritz Jr, Hugo	40%/40%/20%	Detergent	Monoline
3	Jost, Konrad	40%/40%/20%	Detergent, adhesives	Related diversification
4	Non-family	Fragmented/public	Detergent, adhesives, cosmetics	Related diversification

Table 4.2 Generational growth strategies: Bonnier

Generation	Leader	Ownership	Business	Strategy
1	Gerhard	100%	Book retailing	Monoline
2	Albert	100%	Book publishing	Backward integration
3	Karl Otto	100%	Book + paper publishing	Related diversification
4	Tor	54%/2 owners	Book + paper + magazine publishing	Related diversification
5	Albert	18%/4 owners	Book + paper + magazine publishing + furniture, packaging, engineering, ferry, etc.	Unrelated diversification
6–7	Carl-Johan	Fragmented	Media	Related diversification

Table 4.3 Generational growth strategies: Zegna

Generation	Leader	Ownership	Business	Strategy
1	Angelo	100%	Spinning	Monoline
2	Ermenegildo	100%	Spinning + weaving	Forward integration
3	Aldo, Angelo	50%/50%	Spinning + weaving + confection	Forward integration
4	Paolo, Gildo	Fragmented	Spinning + weaving + confection + retail	Forward integration

The three tables display how the different families and different generations applied growth strategies. In the case of Henkel, the first two generations essentially focused on detergents – and as such on the same monoline strategy – but the second generation strongly grew the business from 110 employees to 5,000 over a 25-year period. The third generation then initiated the internationalization and related diversification strategies. The Bonnier group clearly documents the generational strategic evolution by building wisely on previous achievements. The founder took the family into the industry through book retailing, and the second generation laid the foundation for the future publishing dynasty by moving to book publishing. The subsequent two generations each diversified by adding paper publishing and magazine publishing respectively. The fifth generation chose to maintain these businesses and, at the same time, pursue strong growth through unrelated diversification for political reasons. The sixth generation, sensing that the political and economic environment had changed positively, divested the unrelated businesses and returned their focus to the original publishing business and broadened it to include related media businesses.

A particularly clear demonstration of wise business growth is seen in the Zegna Group. The business growth strategy of each succeeding generation maintained the earlier generation's achievements and enhanced them with another distinctive strategic component in the value chain (see Table 4.4) (Schwass, 2005).

Table 4.4 Zegna: Generational business growth strategies

Generation	Growth strategy			
1	Spinning	–	–	–
2	Spinning	+ weaving	–	–
3	Spinning	+ weaving	+ confection	–
4	Spinning	+ weaving	+ confection	+ retail

This example of vertical integration, with each generation adding another component in the value chain, is powerful because it demonstrates an effective linkage of successful historic achievements with new growth opportunities. The evolutionary approach implies that the previous generations' achievements are still valid and recognized, thereby creating a basis for intergenerational trust and family harmony. This positive spirit facilitates the entrepreneurial growth which in turn validates the achievements of the next generation as successful entrepreneurs in their own right.

Planning for wise business growth

Wise business growth produces multiple and strong benefits. While it is largely up to the next-generation leader to assume the leadership initiative and successfully implement a growth strategy which is both meaningful and adapted to the needs of all interest levels, planning wise growth for the next generation can be seen as the ultimate key responsibility of the senior generation. Third-generation leaders in the Zegna Group launched a strategic experiment with a first shop in Paris which did not progress for five years. The experiment, however, provided a learning experience for the family and management which ultimately created the platform for the fourth generation to successfully move into retailing. The concept was available when the fourth generation arrived; they then took emotional ownership of it and very successfully implemented it. From the perspective of the senior generation, setting up strategic experiments for the next-generation business growth opportunities should be a primary concern. This is particularly true when they are in the "let do" phase and concerned with institutional leadership planning. Typically, however, most senior-generation family leaders undertake strong efforts to ensure preservation of past and current strategies. Instead, research on the award-winning family businesses highlights that throughout multiple generations many different efforts were undertaken by senior generations to plan for an evolutionary growth strategy in the next generation. Sam Johnson's father gave his son the responsibility of a newly created department for the development of new products, which became the platform for a strong diversification growth strategy very successfully implemented by Sam. The Zegna fourth generation, realizing that their generation's retail strategy of a vertically integrated value chain for men's clothing could not be expanded, acquired a business in women's fashion. The much larger number of family members growing up in the fifth generation may find their own business growth opportunities in this market, which is new for the Group.

Wise business growth effectively links tradition with innovation. Understanding tradition is a key task for an aspiring next-generation leader. Obtaining this understanding requires formal and informal interaction with the senior generation and thereby raises their comfort and trust level, which enhances the sense of harmony amongst the family. Adopting a growth strategy for the business requires courage, the willingness to take calculated risks and a healthy sense of self-confidence by the new leader. A very visible example is provided through the five generations of the Hermès family where each generation leveraged the earlier generations' achievements and tradition for another creative and innovative product addition. Today's leather belts, bags and wallets apply the same complicated stitching style which the founder successfully brought to saddle making in 1837. The same attention to detail and highest possible quality is applied to the silk scarves introduced by the fourth generation. Being able to benchmark with the historic quality and also risk profile of the family business over several generations greatly facilitates the task of a leader and leads to a greater belief in and commitment to the growth strategy. There are interesting examples of patterns for risk taking amongst the award-winning family businesses. The Bonnier family, in the third generation, acquired a publishing firm that was valued at more than the value of the Bonniers' assets. Similar types of high-risk decisions can be observed in its subsequent generations. Most recently, in the sixth generation, the family took publicly traded Marieberg private.

In summary, growing the business in a wise way is effective both for the long-term survival as a family business and for the new leader's sense of self-worth and personal market value as a proven achiever.

Business growth strategies: risks and opportunities

Risk A. A key risk in not implementing an evolutionary growth strategy in the next generation is that the family's attitude towards tradition and past success and achievements becomes too entrenched. Most families tend to be too backwards oriented in their assessment of business strategy. This is particularly true if the business has a large number of inactive family members who are more distant from it and who have a conservative risk profile. Change, even if evolutionary, often brings out fear of the unknown. Change may also be interpreted as implicit criticism of the previous generation's achievements, thus potentially creating intergenerational conflict.

Opportunity A. The successful implementation of wise business growth strategies in each generation is best achieved by attracting qualified independent advice, either on the board level or as consultants. The non-family advisors provide a neutral evaluation of the business' opportunities and requirements. Industry experts may provide perspectives and knowledge which the family may not possess. This knowledge must be transmitted in an adequate form to as many family members as practical. A transparent educational and informational process builds understanding and support for necessary and meaningful changes.

Risk B. Another key risk is the real or perceived need for additional capital to fund business growth. Growing families with an increasing number of inactive family members may fear that the business may not generate sufficient funding for both growth and dividends. In these cases, most families tend to forgo business growth opportunities.

Opportunity B. Business growth does not necessarily require additional or substantial funding. This may be a good opportunity to steer the business into a new direction, one that provides higher value added with lower capital investment requirements. The expansion of the Zegna Group into retailing was largely financed through franchising and initially only about one third of the stores were operated under direct Zegna ownership. This strategic expansion was entirely internally financed. Another strategic opportunity is to restructure the existing business as a subsidiary of a new holding company that is totally controlled by the family. The subsidiary may be opened up to outside investors to fund important growth, while the family retains ownership control of the holding company. This permits investments in other business projects, thus, creating a portfolio of business subsidiaries that may be expanded or sold according to market opportunities. As a result, the original family business shifts into the broader based concept of a "family in business".

5
Conclusion

Family businesses are complex structures; they have to reconcile and create equilibrium for the needs of four different interest levels: family, ownership, management and the individual. Over time, the needs of these four stakeholders change and evolve, thereby creating the need for a new equilibrium. Most family businesses experience difficulties in finding an effective approach in creating the new equilibrium, which results in high financial and human opportunity costs. The nine award-winning family businesses provide insights and examples for meaningful and effective solutions. Most importantly, they actively developed the next-generation leaders. This is by far the most important strategic decision a family – as business owners – faces in regard to sustaining the family business.

This book has analysed the complex challenges faced by family business leaders over a lifecycle. Leadership is presented as a three-phased model. Each phase experiences changing needs from the four interest levels: family, ownership, management and the individual. Understanding the evolutionary needs of the business allows the formulation of an effective development strategy for the next-generation leader. For long-term effectiveness, this strategy must consider and address the needs in an anticipatory and dynamic mode. Best practices drawn from the award-winning family businesses point towards a three-dimensional growth strategy for leadership development. Firstly, the next-generation leader indicates the willingness to develop and grow as a responsible individual. Secondly, a systematic and transparent process is applied in growing their role in the business. Thirdly, a business growth strategy is implemented which actively builds on previous generations' achievements and meaningfully links those achievements with innovation. This three-dimensional leadership development embodies the concept of "wise growth".

"Wise growth" builds on understanding the real complexities within the evolutionary framework of the four interest levels. It brings to the forefront the human dimension in the family business – the family as the ultimate driver of the business. The family begins with a shared vision for the future. Over time, those family members, who eventually develop diverging visions and aspirations, leave. Those who remain subscribe to a wise growth strategy that enables a capable next-generation leader to emerge. A well-planned and transparent process builds trust during the development phase and beyond. The answer to the "why" question – "Why continue the family business?" – is ultimately found here: understanding the real needs of the individual and the families and addressing them effectively within a transparent set of structures and processes.

The award-winning family businesses are examples of family businesses that have managed to adapt when necessary, and have done so effectively. The ability to look backwards, when necessary, with a clear focus on the future is the base of their wise-growth strategies – and the reason for their successful growth for multiple generations.

In researching and writing this book, I gained many insights into what makes family businesses successful. I have attempted to describe a systematic and practical approach on how to develop successive generations of family business leaders and a meaningful process that a family member, who wants to become the business leader, can follow in order to grow as an individual, grow in their role, and finally, grow the business. It is my hope that other family businesses will learn and benefit from the wise-growth concept of the award-winning families.

Appendix A: Family Business – an Important, Developing Field of Research

The academic world of family business is fascinating in a number of respects. Firstly, it is one of the youngest academic disciplines. It was launched in the 1980s in the United States and eventually migrated to Europe as a serious research topic by the end of the 1980s. What is fascinating about this late emergence as an academic field is the fact that family businesses, without doubt, are the oldest form of business organization. Family businesses can be traced back over 2,000 years: Jesus Christ was mentioned as having worked in his father's family business.

The oldest surviving family businesses are found in Japan: a cabinet-making family firm founded in the sixth century, Kongo Gumi, and the Hoshi Hotel, founded in 718 and still owned and managed by the 46th generation of direct descendants of the founding family. The latter is part of "The Henokians", a Paris, France, based association of about 30 family businesses over 200 years old. To belong to this exclusive club, the family business must be majority owned and managed by descendants of the founding family and the business must be financially sound. It is noteworthy that a large proportion of the members are active in wine and spirit making. The attachment of families to property is a common trait of many of the oldest surviving family businesses.

On the one hand the family business is the oldest form of corporate organization; on the other, it is a very young academic discipline. Why has comprehensive research into family businesses only recently begun?

One answer may be that the academic world's traditional deep specialization is not adapted to the needs of interdisciplinary fields. And this is precisely what family business research needs, an interdisciplinary approach which encompasses a number of disciplines: general management, ownership, leadership, sociology, psychology, anthropology – the list is exhaustive. Another way of stating the problem is that family businesses need the understanding of the "softer" dimension of the "family" system on the one hand, and the "harder" dimension of the "business" system, on the other. Linking those two contrary structures is by no means an automatic or easy process. In fact, it took – and still does – market driven initiatives to create the base for comprehensive research on an interdisciplinary approach. There are many examples of both US- and European-based academic research centres and chairs which were launched as the result of family business financial endowments and gifts. The family business research and educational activities at IMD were made possible in 1988 by the endowment of Stephan Schmidheiny, a well-known Swiss family business entrepreneur. Subsequently, Thierry Lombard, of the 200-year-old private bank Lombard Odier Darier Hentsch in Geneva, initiated the creation of the dedicated Family Business Research Center at IMD. In the US, most of the over 100 family business centres carry the names of the family businesses that provided the initial financial sponsorship.

A second reason why there is only recent research may be found in family businesses themselves. Family businesses are typically very discreet – if not secretive. Few family businesses have allowed outsiders to study them, especially in regard to the interaction between the separate realms of the family and the business. This aversion to openness and transparency has discouraged many research efforts and made it more difficult to create a systematic analysis of success strategies, in particular.

The third fascinating characteristic of family businesses is their enormous macroeconomic importance. Their importance is undisputed whichever definition of family business is adopted. So far, there is no commonly accepted and agreed upon definition of who qualifies as a family business. Most definitions focus on a quantitative ownership approach, linking a given family to a controlling ownership stake. A more realistic approach reduces the weight of the quantifiable ownership in favour of the qualitative element of the family influence over the business, especially for its future orientation. This more qualitative approach means that the family plays a key role – directly or indirectly – in appointing the CEO. Family businesses do not require absolute ownership control in order to be able to select the CEO.

When this broader definition of family business is adopted, surveys conducted in a number of countries indicate that typically family businesses represent the largest percentage of all registered companies, from just over half in the Netherlands to almost all in Italy. While these numbers are impressive, one real indicator of the strength of family businesses is measured by their contribution to the gross national product (GNP) which is estimated at 45–70 per cent. Another is their contribution to the rate of employment of the overall workforce. A major turning point for the recognition of family business importance came in May 2000, when the European Community officially, and for the first time, published their findings, whereby European family businesses employed 45 million workers.

The fourth fascinating characteristic of family businesses is that not only are they significant contributors to national economies, but they also tend to outperform other forms of corporate organizations. In 2003, the *Journal of Finance* published a research study that indicated that family businesses are clearly more profitable than publicly traded corporations. Several earlier studies have also pointed in this direction.

Combining the element of significant macroeconomic importance with the superior competitive performance of family businesses leads to an increasing level of interest in the strengths of this particular form of business organization. One barometer for this is the strong annual increase in the number of research papers presented at the Annual World Conference of the Family Business Network (FBN), the world's premier association of family businesses.

Appendix B: Distinguished Family Business Award

IMD, in partnership with Lombard Odier Darier Hentsch, awards the Distinguished Family Business Award.

The award was created in 1996 in order to meet the following objectives:

- To highlight the important global economic contribution of family businesses
- To recognize, annually, an outstanding company which has successfully blended family and business interests
- To identify best practices which may be useful to other family businesses.

A distinguished award committee was formed in order to first nominate and then select the annual award-winner. This committee is comprised of over 20 leading family business owners and academics from all over the world.

At the beginning of each year, the committee members nominate candidates which follow these criteria:

1. To have reached at least the third generation of family ownership and management
2. To have achieved a solid long-term record of financial performance and stability
3. To produce products which are market leaders and respected in their industry segment
4. To have established and maintained an effective governance system
5. To be an international business
6. To have effectively linked tradition and innovation
7. To have demonstrated good corporate citizenship by making a social contribution to the communities within which it operates.

The nominated firms are submitted to a rigorous in-depth analysis with respect to their qualification for each of the seven criteria. This research is conducted by the IMD family business research team. The research team also draws on qualified outside evaluations and opinions. The award committee has the final word on the selection of the annual award-winner. The process is conducted independent of the IMD President and the Lombard Odier Darier Hentsch Managing Partners.

The award winners are announced each year at the gala dinner of the Annual Family Business Network World Conference. This is the most respected annual educational and networking event for leading family businesses from all over the world. The award winner receives a trophy which is crafted by Chopard of Geneva, a family-owned and managed luxury watch and jewellery firm. A presentation of the winning family business precedes a plenary interview with delegates from the family business. An in-depth article explaining the historic evolution of the award winner is usually broadly published.

Distinguished Family Business Award Winners – 1996–2004

1996 Lego Group, Denmark
1997 Hermès SA, France
1998 Corporacion Puig, Spain
1999 Henkel Group, Germany
2000 Zegna Group, Italy
2001 Murugappa Group, India
2002 Samuel C. Johnson Family Enterprises, US
2003 Bonnier Group, Sweden
2004 Barilla Group, Italy

Appendix C: The Articles on the Nine Award-Winning Family Businesses

The following articles were published in the year of the respective award.

The LEGO Group

IMD Distinguished Family Business Award Winner 1996
By Jonathan Pellegrin, Executive-in-Residence, Family Business Area at IMD

Founded in 1932, the LEGO Group, with close to 9,000 employees all over the world, has consistently blended business and family interests successfully. There are many lessons family businesses can learn through reviewing the following best practices identified by IMD's Distinguished Family Business Award selection panel during their research of the LEGO Group:

Prudent risk taking and conservative financial management

During the Great Depression of the 1930s, financial catastrophes faced by the fledgling carpentry company's customers nearly forced the founder and his business into bankruptcy. Recognizing that people could not afford to build houses, Ole Kirk Christiansen reinvented his business and began producing stepladders, ironing boards and wooden toys. Demand for the well-made toys (called LEGO – a combination of two Danish words "*leg godt*" meaning "play well") was strong, and new products were developed. Ironically, the diversification that was created to save the company, in fact, became the company. Christiansen believed that producing very high quality, less expensive products with more stable consumption levels would protect his company against future economic downturns.

The financial problems caused by the depression, along with some early management difficulties, persuaded the family to embrace a conservative attitude toward their balance sheet. The family felt a deep sense of responsibility to both their employees and vendors and early on developed a reputation for honouring their financial obligations.

Concentration and focus on full exploitation of core product line

In 1949, the company introduced a primitive forerunner of what was to become the revolutionary plastic building bricks. These toy construction components were popular and represented an opportunity for significant growth.

In 1955, the founder's son, Godtfred Kirk Christiansen, recognized that the children's toy market was primarily comprised of "one-off" products. He filled what was perceived as a market gap by launching the "LEGO System of Play" based on the building bricks. The concept involved development and packaging of a starter kit followed by the systematic addition of new elements and play themes. This product development cascade was designed to stimulate greater retail commitment of shelf space and more time spent with the product and additional purchases by consumers.

Considering that just six of the original eight studded bricks of the same colour can be put together in 102,981,500 different ways, the opportunities for creative play are virtually limitless. Every year, more than 100 new LEGO sets are added to the range, and around the same number are withdrawn. New elements, play themes and sets result from the hundreds of ideas that come out of six product development departments in Denmark, the US and Japan.

Engender interest of next generation in the family business at an early age

Godtfred Kirk Christiansen, the founder's son, began working in the company when he was only 12 years old and literally grew up in the company. By the age of 18, he was designing new toy models. At age 24, he had become his father's right-hand man, responsible for product development, sales and finance. He gradually assumed more and more responsibility for managing the business as his father's health declined.

From an early age, GKC's son, Kjeld Kirk Kristiansen[1] developed a reputation as a skilled and imaginative LEGO builder. GKC looked to young Kjeld as a great source of product development ideas. Upon completion of his upper-secondary education, Kjeld joined the staff of the Group's German subsidiary as a trainee. He then took a commercial degree in Denmark, followed by an MBA in 1972. During his studies, he gradually realized what role he wanted to play in the family business.

The first two generations, Ole and then Godtfred Christiansen, did five important things in developing their sons for the business:

1. They exposed their sons to the business at a very early age
2. They provided their sons with opportunities to work on meaningful projects as soon as they began working in the company
3. After giving their sons actual working experience in the company, the sons went away to school for further education and training
4. They gave their sons significant responsibilities and allowed them to succeed or fail in a visible way
5. They gave their sons the opportunity to increase their responsibilities at a rapid rate and grow professionally while still very young and full of enthusiasm for the business.

Hire a non-family executive to assist with generational management transitions

Vagn Holck Andersen, a seasoned Danish executive, was consulting with Godtfred about the possible sale of the LEGO Group following the tragic death of his daughter in an automobile accident. Holck advised GKC not to sell the company, and was consequently hired as senior vice-president, reporting to GKC, responsible for maintaining control over the rapidly growing organization.

Andersen's role over his entire career became one of being the "buffer" between father and son. Throughout his involvement with the LEGO Group, Andersen was a key contributor to the decision-making processes and facilitated the dialogue between father and son so decisions were made objectively, not emotionally. He retired in 1996 as chairman of the parent company.

Global expansion should begin close to home with familiar products

The globalization of the LEGO Group was nearly as systematic as the development and expansion of the product line. Beginning in neighbouring Norway, distribution was expanded throughout Europe. Subsequently, captive sales companies were established around the world. By the early 1970s, the LEGO Group had truly become a well-known global brand.

An outside, professional board stretches and challenges the CEO

When Kjeld Kirk Kristiansen received the IMD Distinguished Family Business Award, he said: "To have a strong and active board was not even considered in my grandfather's time, and as to my father, he wanted to have a board, although at the same time, he didn't really want to use it. For me, however, it has been very important to work closely together with an active and professional board. Especially when it comes to involving the board members as sparring partners for discussing new concepts and strategies."

Today, the board of directors of LEGO Group A/S includes two executives from large, multinational public companies, one of which is family controlled, the non-family CEO of a very large multinational family-owned company, the Kristiansen family lawyer and Kjeld's brother-in-law representing the family ownership outside of Kjeld's family.

Good corporate citizenship creates a better business environment

All of the LEGO Group's business activities have followed the guiding principle that it must be a good corporate citizen. The company has been recognized throughout the world for the positive contributions it has made to the development of young people through LEGO products as well as the contributions it has made to the communities in which it operates.

Billund, Denmark, has a modern, efficient international airport served by commercial airlines thanks to the LEGO Group, which donated it to the community. It is the second largest airport in Denmark. In 1985, the LEGO Group founded an annual international prize which now awards DKr. 1 million to individuals and/or groups which have: developed a wider knowledge of the conditions under which children live and grow up; promoted children's welfare and development; made an outstanding educational effort for the benefit of children or helped generate a broader understanding of children, their situation and conditions.

The company carries out regular educational initiatives dedicated to preserving the environment, and it has been recognized and honoured for developing and adopting environmentally sensitive manufacturing and production processes.

Take time for a sabbatical; it can renew and refresh the company

An effective way for a family CEO to get refreshed and renewed is to periodically get away from the business and take a sabbatical. In Kjeld Kristiansen's case, after 15 years as president of the LEGO Group, a prolonged illness resulted in an unplanned sabbatical.

It proved, however, to be fortunate. Having sustained growth for more than four decades and continuous improvement in its systems approach, the company had nearly "written the book on success". There were, however, many things going on in the LEGO markets to which it was not reacting because of its tradition of success and bureaucratic management.

While Kjeld was convalescing, he realized that as LEGO markets were undergoing major changes due to globalization, information technology, the media revolution and related new lifestyles; therefore the approach of LEGO management would also have to change. The historic drive for consensus had led to a very system- and plan-oriented organization which had lost the necessary dynamism and entrepreneurship to effectively compete in the new world order.

Initial thinking during Kjeld's forced sabbatical led him to implement "Compass Management (CM)", a new management direction at the LEGO Group, upon his return. Under CM the company has embarked on a process of changing attitudes and behaviour of employees (see Table A1).

Table A1 Compass Management: a process of changing attitudes and behaviours

From looking at details and doing things right	➢ to looking at perspective and doing the right things
From internal focus	➢ to consumer focus
From consensus and long debates	➢ to commitment, empowerment and action
From slow reaction	➢ to fast action
From individual and functional mindset	➢ to a shared global mindset, shared values, shared objectives and a shared direction for the future development of the company

The current generation's perspective

During recent conversations with IMD faculty, Kjeld Kristiansen said: "The long term reinvention of our company through 'Compass Management' has implications for just about everything we do. It is not an easy or short-term project in a company, which has always been accustomed to success. It is the introduction of a whole new way of thinking, which we believe will carry us successfully into the next millennium. Through three generations of family ownership and family management, the LEGO Group has grown from a small workshop into a global company aiming at being the world's most respected and esteemed brand among families with children."

Note

1. Kjeld Kirk Kristiansen's name was officially misspelled during registry and he took no steps to change the mistake.

Hermès

IMD Distinguished Family Business Award Winner 1997
By Professor Joachim Schwass, IMD Industry Professor, and Dr Monica Wagen, IMD Research Associate

Known as one of the world's most elegant businesses, Hermès SA is a French manufacturer and marketer of upmarket luggage, apparel and accessories. From a nineteenth-century foundation in leather goods, the company has since diversified into silk goods (about 25 per cent of revenues in 1996), ready-to-wear clothing (13 per cent), watches (10 per cent) and perfumes (7.5 per cent). Its ongoing dedication to family ownership and management, impeccable craftsmanship, and careful protection of the brand's mystique set Hermès apart from most other companies.

Family businesses can learn many valuable lessons by reviewing the following best practices identified by IMD's Distinguished Family Business Award selection panel during the research of the Hermès group.

Expanding internationally

From the late 1980s until today, Hermès has been led by Jean-Louis Dumas, a fifth-generation descendant of the founder. He has been credited with building Hermès' worldwide retailing empire by directing an intense programme of geographic expansion. Although more than 50 per cent of annual sales were still generated in Europe in the 1990s, the Asia/Pacific region contributed nearly one third of annual revenues, and the US pitched in 11 per cent of yearly turnover. From 1986 to 1996, Hermès enjoyed average annual sales increases of 24 per cent.

Developing a product line

During the 1970s, some observers feared that Hermès' profitability was being sacrificed on the altar of quality. The concern was that, with the arrival of non-man-made materials like plastic and polyester and the growing vogue for easy-going styles, the Hermès dedication to classic, natural materials (silk and leather) and modest styles could lose impact. And effectively, the usual Hermès 5 per cent annual sales growth started to drop.

To overcome the crisis, the company hired new clothing designers to revive the apparel line and develop new items, like motorcycle jackets and fantasy jeans. In 1979, a French advertising campaign that featured a young woman wearing a Hermès scarf introduced the branded goods to a new generation of consumers. This move changed the Hermès label from the object of an older generation's nostalgia to the subject of young people's dreams. By 1990, Hermès had expanded its line of merchandise to include 30,000 different items.

Creating an image of quality

The company's explosive growth – annual sales grew from US$50 million in 1978 to US$700 million by 1996, and its net profit grew even faster – had as much to do with changing consumer values as the revitalization of Hermès strategy. The company took advantage of the resurgence in Hermès popularity by boosting store locations and licensed boutiques in America, Japan, Asia and the Pacific. The number of Hermès-owned stores quadrupled from 15 in 1978 to 80 in 1996, as the total number of outlets worldwide grew to more than 225. In recent years, the demand for the products has increased beyond all expectations – the company is planning to develop new markets, in three to five years, to have 30 fully owned Hermès stores in Asia and ten in the US.

Developing "market leader" products

Some observers consider Hermès scarves collectible works of art. Overall scarf volume increased by 250,000 in 1978 to 1.2 million in 1989. Hermès' combination of quality materials and time-consuming hand craftsmanship was reflected in its high retail prices. By the mid-1990s, one Hermès scarf commanded US$245, a tie cost US$115, and a "Kelly" purse set cost about US$3,500.

Transmitting the company successfully through five generations

Hermès' trademark – a horse-drawn carriage – harkens back to its original saddlery business.

- Founded in 1837 by Thierry Hermès, the firm gained a reputation as a producer of one-of-a-kind saddlery for European noblemen. The functional and decorative "saddle stitch" used by Hermès craftsmen to join pieces of leather would come to represent the branded goods' quality and simple elegance. Throughout the 19th and 20th centuries, the company continued to custom-make saddles, investing 20 to 40 hours in each.
- In the 1870s, the founder transmitted the business to his son Emile-Charles Hermès, who moved the business to the rue du Faubourg St Honoré, a site that would become one of Paris' most prized pieces of real estate. After a few years at the helm, Emile-Charles sold his stake in the business to his son Emile-Maurice in 1922.
- Faced with the ascent of the automobile and corresponding obsolescence of the carriage, Emile-Maurice Hermès began to diversify into travel- and sports-related leather goods, but he never abandoned Hermès' "horsy heritage". Saddlebags gave way to luggage, wallets and handbags. For instance, the famous Hermès "Kelly" bag, named in the 1950s after Princess Grace of Monaco, who was often photographed with the accessory, helped burnish the brand image as an accoutrement for royalty and celebrities. In the early 1920s, Emile-Maurice bought a patent from the Canadian inventor of the zipper, and brought it back to France. The zipper became so closely associated with Hermès products like handbags, jockey silks and leather goods that Frenchmen came to call the invention "La fermeture Hermès".

In the 1920s, the company launched ready-to-wear clothing, leather-banded watches and leather gloves.
- In the 1930s, Emile-Maurice passed the family business on to his son-in-law, Robert Dumas. (This transmission meant that in the fourth generation, the Hermès name was no longer carried on by the CEO, but by the female line.) Robert directed the design and production of the first Hermès scarf in 1937. Over the years, the scarves became ingrained in the European culture as a traditional heirloom. Although scarf production slackened in the mid-twentieth century, by the mid-1980s, Hermès was unveiling a dozen new designs each year.
- In 1978, Jean-Louis Dumas, the fourth of six children, took over the company's top position after the death of his father. He had first worked as a buyer for competitors before returning to the family firm in 1964. This "outside" experience was certainly the catalyst for the sweeping turnaround he engineered in the 1980s.

Creating a strong financial structure (going public)

Based on family consensus, Hermès made its first stock offering in June 1993. But the family retained over 80 per cent of the equity in the hands of 56 family members, six of whom kept a 5–10 per cent stake. The 425,000 shares floated at US$55 and were oversubscribed by a factor of 34. Ultimately, there were approximately 4,000 outside shareholders. Actually, the equity sale helped lessen family tensions by allowing some members to liquidate their holdings without squabbling among themselves over share valuations. With the share flotation, family members could have shares with a fluctuating value, an established price, liquidity, and, if they wanted to buy houses or cars, they could do so without affecting the market. In the eyes of the owning family, going public increased stability while still keeping a strong family influence. They consider themselves a public company with a "Fort Knox-type" family culture.

Developing strong family/business relationships

The family firm is, according to the owners, based on the principle of a democratic monarchy. This means that the owners have:

- Strong leadership, in the person of the CEO, closely related to the family body (more than 40 family members in the sixth generation)
- Several members of the three branches (Dumas, Puech and Guerrand) of the family work in the company at different levels
- A structure to keep family influence thanks to a strategy committee of several family representatives, with shared responsibility
- A board of directors composed mainly of family members
- Written company regulations and a family constitution with rules for selling and buying shares, with limited family voting rights, and so on, was established after Hermès went public
- To avoid the dilution of the voting rights, non-family buyers and the divorced family members can have shares, but no voting rights
- A 75 per cent majority is needed to change the company statutes as well as the CEO, so as to keep family influence

- The next generation is directly immersed in the tradition of the company at an early age – regular, organized tours to subsidiaries and company suppliers give them a stronger feeling for the product and its creation.

Cultivating strong values

The owning family wants Hermès to remain a family firm. They believe it is desirable, but not imperative, that the CEO be a family member. What is imperative to them is that the family shareholders choose this person. They believe the family should have majority control in the ordinary and extraordinary meetings. In their opinion, if the family does not have that control, even if the CEO has been appointed by the family, the company would lose part of its family character. They believe that the family has few rights and many obligations. These obligations are part of the family culture and ethic. Among other values, Hermès stipulates:

- Respect for people and nature. Towards nature they feel not so much admiration but gratitude. What would Hermès be without the silkworms to spin their cocoons, or the cattle to provide leather?
- Respect for new ideas. At every level, Hermès has always stimulated new ideas and the desire for perfection.

Stimulating company culture

All the human elements that together make up Hermès have a remarkably strong identification with and pride in the firm. To give an example of this pride, a doctor who has many patients in the company commented that when he asked other patients what jobs they had, they replied that they were secretaries, engineers, and so on. The employees of Hermès, however, say, "I am with Hermès." All these people seem to be united in their love for quality, and their creative vitality contributes greatly to the company's family spirit.

Developing financial autonomy

Hermès was able, despite being risk takers, to stick to the principle of self-financing. To avoid financial dependence on the banks, but still have the capital needed for new projects, Hermès traditionally reinvests approximately 15 per cent of the profits in the company.

Stimulating family pride

According to Jean-Louis Dumas,

> The secret of our company lies in a job well done. Everyone should be proud of doing his or her best. This type of pride is not arrogance, but tempered by humility and shared enthusiasm. You are more proud thinking that your grandchildren will harvest the fruit of your labours. The only valid criterion of their satisfaction is whether if, thanks to some miracle, their grandfather returned to life, he would pat them on the back and tell them that they have done a good job. The main idea is that yesterday's ship is ancestral and it is our duty to conserve it even though we did not build it. Today, every family member is responsible for one of the oars.

Corporacion Puig

IMD Distinguished Family Business Award Winner 1998
By Dr Monica Wagen, IMD

Long viewed as a prestigious company, the Barcelona-based Corporacion Puig is one of the few remaining family-owned perfume and fashion houses. Its various activities range from mass-market products with brand names such as Agua Lavanda Puig, Aqua Brava and Quorum, to world-renowned brands such as Carolina Herrera, Paco Rabanne and Nina Ricci. Puig's product lines include fashion goods, haute couture, perfumes, as well as L'Air du temps from Nina Ricci, which is one of the world's top ten fragrances. Herrera for Men and Paco Rabanne Pour Homme are already considered classic perfumes. With growth rates of 15 per cent in the last five years, Corporacion Puig has been regularly increasing its market position, thanks to the development of prestigious branded products.

This year, Corporacion Puig is the winner of the prestigious Distinguished Family Business Award given by IMD. The Award, given each year to a family business (LEGO, Denmark, in 1996 and Hermès, Paris, in 1997) recognizes the Spanish company for its remarkable geographic expansion. The award also recognizes the family's ongoing dedication to family management and ownership, which sets Corporacion Puig apart from most other companies. Family businesses can learn many valuable lessons from the following Corporacion Puig practices identified by IMD's research.

The Puig Company's development

At the turn of the twentieth century, Antonio Puig established a small perfumery company, with distribution throughout Spain.

Later, he began manufacturing his own products, and when he became the first Spanish lipstick manufacturer, he caused something of a social outcry. According to Puig family legend, in making lipstick, Antonio Puig encountered problems with the packaging and went to see his supplier. The supplier's response was, "If you help me financially, I'll be able to find a solution."

To gain better control of the production chain, Puig acquired the supplier's entire plant and started diversification. This purchase was the first breakpoint in Corporacion Puig's history. It launched a series of mergers and acquisitions that ultimately brought the company, which had been limited to a niche market, to a position of leadership in the fashion industry.

Founder's legacy

Antonio Puig, Corporacion Puig's founder, had four children. He gave them an adequate education and encouraged them to be active in the business. The first, Antonio Puig Jr, and the second, Mariano, entered the flagship company, the perfumery business. The third developed the company's diversification activity. And the fourth had the position of institutional relations and communications director. The second generation thus grew up and came to occupy their individual positions. But they still felt very strong family bonds. In 1979, Antonio fell ill, and on his deathbed, he left his four children a legacy and testament that still guides the family, "Stay together. Your unity will be your strength." This "unity" has been one of the identifying characteristics of the second generation. Formal and informal meetings take place among the members of the second generation, communication is excellent, and respect for one another abounds.

New direction

Even as far back as the mid-twentieth century, following the principles of primogeniture and consensus, the flagship company gradually came under the direction of a twosome: the founder's first and second children, Antonio Jr and Mariano. In the early 1950s, the duo established five major objectives: team work, product creation, internationalization, critical mass, and effective internal organization.

To meet these objectives – in fact, to survive as a company – Puig had to create a fashionable, attractive product. To give their product the market presence and image it needed, the Puigs approached the most talented designers. With this move, the company was the first in the perfume industry to work with industrial designers and famous artists. They then created a packaging development office and an R&D laboratory to define the content, in order to be able to obtain the best raw materials and to create the best product. Since that time, one of the company's trademarks has been its extraordinary concern for quality and excellence.

Early internationalization

Once the two managers had the right product, they saw that Puig's all-important research and development expenditures could not be recouped from a market the size of Spain. So they went international. (This happened 35 years ago, when international expansion was still uncommon in Spain.) The company set up a venture in the US to sell Puig's Spanish product. But it quickly became apparent that the Spanish product was not attractive enough for the US market.

Puig needed a product with a Parisian label. So they created a company in Paris, with its own product development, its own marketing, and its own funds, with French personnel, and fully dependent on its own industry. In succession, they then built distribution companies in Britain, Germany, Holland, Central America, South America, the Middle East and other regions.

Keep in mind that not even ten years ago, Corporacion Puig's competition was basically small- to medium-sized family-owned businesses bearing the name of the founder: for example, Christian Dior, Helena Rubinstein, and Yves Saint-Laurent. Today, however, Corporacion Puig has seven large competitors who, little by little, have bought out these other companies and now control a very high market percentage and command seemingly infinite financial resources.

A strict dividend policy

In the 1970s, the two managers from the second generation realized that internal growth was insufficient to reach the critical mass needed to compete against the leading international groups. They had no choice but to create a financial infrastructure to collect resources. So in order to have the necessary liquidity but stay independent, they established strict rules to limit the distribution of dividends. These rules may have asked the family to make sacrifices, but they enabled the company to grow by purchasing famous brand names that showed distinct potential for expansion.

Making management professional

Creating the structure for international expansion meant completely reorganizing the management. To this point, the general management had directed each of the group's companies. Basically, the family was directing the family's flagship. Nevertheless, it was decided that the family needed to move up to a higher level. A general director was needed – even though it would cost them. So the family promoted Javier Cano, an industrial engineer with 25 years' experience in various company positions, to be the new CEO of the flagship. This sent a strong message of career opportunities for non-family managers. And since Cano's age put him between the two generations, his appointment also set up a valuable link between them.

The third generation: strong family/business relationship

As the family grew to four brothers in the second generation and to 14 cousins in the third generation, things grew more complicated. The second generation already had top positions in the holding company, but was not involved in day-to-day affairs. Although some of the firstborn of the third generation had moved on to executive positions, they realized that, with 18 shareholders, it was impossible to work as they had with four. Clearly, the system needed to be changed.

So to maintain family involvement, they restructured by creating a governing system made up of the assembly of shareholders, the holding (which embraces the various companies), the family council and the advisory board, as follows:

1. The family council consists of one representative from each branch of the second generation and one representative from the third generation, all older than 30. It meets at least twice a year and otherwise, as necessary. Two standing orders – a family handbook (code of behaviour) and a family protocol – were created by the family council.
2. The assembly of shareholders meets a couple of times a year (convening both those who work in the company and those who do not). Operational matters are explained; comments from attendees are received, so communication between shareholders and management stays open; and an attempt is made to ensure that shareholders remain proud, satisfied members of the group.
3. The holding, the primary mission of which is to be the steward of the group's patrimony, is its financial, strategic, control and management centre. It is composed of four shareholders, one from each family branch, the same four people who are involved in the advisory board, each having one vote.

4. Another organ is the advisory board. There has always been a group of people to whom the family goes for informal advice. At a certain moment, however, it became clear that a more formal vehicle for this informal guidance would be beneficial. The advisory board was established, a total of four people from the family, one member from each branch, and an additional four from outside the family.

Cultivating strong values

The family handbook expresses the Puig family's feelings, as business people and as family members, so the employees can better carry out the intentions of the family. In other words, the book summarizes the moral position, ethics, and professional principles in such a way that any person in the group will know how the owning family thinks and wants things done. For example, a proposal was made regarding a French product bearing the name *"amaigrissant"* (weight reducer). The managers, knowing this was dishonest, did not carry it out – family ethics do not sanction the sale of a product that makes false claims. The family handbook ends by stating that the Puig family wants the company to remain independent and that, therefore, profits must be produced to finance growth.

Family protocol

The family always tries to operate with love (love of parents for their children and love among siblings) and always has the interests of the business in mind. Conscious that these two values may be at odds, family members created a family protocol of unity between the company and the family. The protocol is essentially a series of rules, like the following:

- Family members who come to serve as executives must have university degrees and must have worked for a minimum of five years outside the family company. For instance, Mariano's son is an industrial engineer who works for Nestlé; his nephew works as an economist at Pepsi; one of his nieces is a lawyer and works in a museum of art, and so on. Qualified people like these are on a waiting list, with the expectation that, one day, if the right situation should arise, and if they have proven their professional abilities, the company may call them. This way, these individuals will bring a new cultural outlook into the company.
- In-laws will not form part of the company's executive board.
- No shareholders are allowed to use their shares as collateral for other personal objectives.
- If, at any moment, a member of the family bearing the Puig surname separates from the company, that member shall not produce goods that could compete with the company. On the other hand, the group builds a financial reserve to purchase – at a pre-determined price the shares of a member who wishes to leave.

The list is quite long and changes according to the times and the needs – the family protocol is a "living" document.

Composition of the advisory board

When it came to bringing in external advisors, Corporacion Puig established a desired profile, guided by the following principles:

- Among the people on the advisory board, there should not be any friends, or consultants
- It is important that these people be well remunerated, and that they feel obligated to fulfil their assigned task, not defend their own interests.

Founded on these ideas, the profile of possible advisory board members looks like this: individuals accustomed to being creators or developers of important businesses, with a business and international outlook, an industrial and brand image background, and family business experience with which the family members feel comfortable.

Role of the advisory board

The advisory board meets three or four times a year. To date, it has been remarkably efficient, playing a key role, for example, in the following three situations:

1. During the autarky period, the company diversified in packaging and did quite well nationally. But when Spain became a member of the EEC, these activities were unable to compete. In a meeting with the advisory board, the family was advised to get rid of these companies. This was hard for the family at first because these activities were closely identified with the history of the group, but in the end, the family successfully followed the board's advice.
2. The family was trying to buy a competing company. The executive management team was excited because this would mean that their market share would grow and positioning would be strengthened. The seller, however, kept adding conditions; the management team went along – in retrospect, accepting perhaps a little too lightly. Fortunately, the advisory board stepped in, admonishing them not to meet further conditions. Negotiations broke down. A year went by. The seller came back, and accepted all the conditions that they would otherwise not have been able to impose.
3. The upward growth rate of the Paris-based company (established there in the sixties) slowed dramatically. The second generation was concerned because France was seen as a highly competitive country. They did not know how to reverse the slide. The advisory board said "Send a member from the third generation there." At first the family was against, but in the end, the board prevailed. And the experience has been excellent; so good, in fact, that this scenario was repeated by sending another member of the third generation to the New York subsidiary.

Corporacion Puig has sought to create structures through which problems can be channelled and resolved. It has four institutional bodies that make decisions by consensus or by majority. On top, one of the leitmotivs of the group is that, in order to subsist, it is important to have a very close-knit base of shareholders, a sufficient critical mass of business and a highly efficient executive team.

Current transition of control

As in many family organizations, the Puigs consider that their greatest challenge is to ensure the continuity of the business. Therefore, for the last six years, they have been drawing up an organizational and strategic plan that defines their future objective, which will guide the transition to the next generation.

As of July 1998, the second generation – Antonio Puig and Mariano Puig – officially retired from the operational business. The baton of executive power was handed over to a newly created executive committee called Excom. The Excom has four members, with equal power and equal authority, each in charge of separate units. On the committee are three family members, Manuel, Mariano Jr and Marc Puig (one son of Antonio and two sons of Mariano) and one non-family manager, Javier Cano. Their tasks are set according to a brand division, which coincides with a country division of the group: the business activities in the USA and Canada, Spain, France and the rest of the world have four different bosses.

The Excom is the highest executive organ of the entire group. It works as a team, in the same way that the brothers of the second generation have traditionally worked. Each senior member of the organization reports, according to their position, to an Excom member. The Excom, in turn, is accountable to the board of directors, which will keep Mariano, of the second generation, as its president. His brother, Antonio, is president of the shareholders' assembly.

Two other brothers remain involved in the business, through the board of directors, and as ambassadors of the group in several organizations, such as the association of perfumery manufacturers.

According to the family mission, the Excom will have a clear mandate: take a leap forward, turn Corporacion Puig into a major multinational player, and bring it into an enviable position in the next millennium.

This paper was based on interviews with the president of the Puig Group, Mariano Puig, and several family members, by Dr Monica Wagen, Research Associate, and Professor Joachim Schwass at IMD, as well as company documents. June 1998.

The Henkel Group

IMD Distinguished Family Business Award Winner 1999
By Professor Joachim Schwass

The Henkel Group, with headquarters in Düsseldorf, Germany, is a large family-controlled business active in detergents, chemical products, adhesives, hygiene, and surface technologies. Today, the fourth generation plays an active ownership role. The Henkel Group has been selected as the recipient of the 1999 IMD Distinguished Family Business Award in recognition of its successful blending of family and business interests.

The beginning

The founder of the business was Fritz Henkel, whose father was a schoolteacher in Germany. In 1876, after observing that detergents had arrived on the market and that they could vastly facilitate cleaning and washing in individual households, Fritz Henkel started his modest business activities. He used bleaching soda and started to sell it himself. He became very successful, and soon employed workers and started to expand. By 1899, having managed to develop the business substantially – employing 79 workers – Henkel required a new location and thus moved outside Düsseldorf. His entrepreneurial ambition was clearly demonstrated by the size of the land he purchased for the future development: 54,846 square metres!

In 1907, Henkel launched the first branded detergent product under the name Persil. He understood that the users wanted a product of consistent quality, and by branding it, Henkel wanted to provide a quality guarantee. He also observed that supplying detergents in bulk was impractical for individual households. He therefore launched the first prepackaged detergent in a smaller household size. Both the branding and the packaging laid the groundwork for the future growth of the company.

In 1908, Henkel started the first conveyor belt packaging line for Persil products: four female workers produced 28 cartons of Persil products per minute. In 1911, employment surged to 925, and the company built the first homes for the workers.

In 1918, Fritz Henkel celebrated his 70th birthday and created a pension fund for the workers. In the same year, the company reduced the daily working hours to eight, with a total working week of 48 hours. After World War I, the detergent manufacturer faced a shortage of raw materials: it became difficult to purchase cardboard and adhesives for the packaging of the detergents. So Fritz Henkel started making these products.

The next generations

Fritz Henkel had three children: Hugo, Fritz Jr, and one daughter, Emmy. The sons were brought into the business while the daughter stayed with her family, as was the tradition then. As unconventional as Fritz Henkel was in his role as a full-blooded entrepreneur, he was just as unconventional – for that time, at least – in his approach to company ownership: he divided the ownership of his business among his three children. Since Emmy was not active in the business, she received 20 per cent ownership; the sons got 40 per cent each. Thereby the three family branches were created, and even today, reference is still made to the "Hugo branch", the "Fritz Jr branch" and the "Emmy branch". The legacy of the founder to his children was that they must stay united as a family in the business.

So far as company operations went, despite the three-way ownership, and with Emmy staying at home, the two brothers assumed the leadership of the company in the classic separation of functions. Hugo became the technical director in 1904; Fritz joined a year later as the commercial director (at that time, the company employed 110 workers).

By 1930, 25 years later, employment had surged to 5,000 workers, with an annual production rate of over 110,000 tons, the vast majority being Persil washing powder. That year, Fritz Henkel Jr unexpectedly passed away, and two months later his father, the founder of the business, Fritz Henkel Sr, died at the age of 81. Hugo assumed sole leadership of the company.

Fritz Jr had had no sons, but Hugo had had three sons and two daughters. Hugo's oldest son, Jost (now the third Henkel generation), was appointed CEO in 1938, with Hugo becoming chairman of the supervisory board. Although two cousins were also active in management positions, they passed away during World War II. So it fell to Jost to rebuild the business after Allied bombing caused widescale destruction. Jost successfully lead the business until 1961, when he, too, died unexpectedly. Until then, the Henkel corporation had focused primarily on building on the foundations Fritz Sr had laid, making and distributing branded and packaged detergents in Germany, with some export activities.

A new era

With the appointment of Konrad Henkel as the head of the company in 1962, the company entered into a major phase of strategic reorientation. Born in 1915, Konrad was Jost's younger brother. A chemist by training, he had devoted his efforts in the business to research and development, so he already had a profound knowledge of Henkel's products when he was asked to lead the company at the age of 46. Konrad felt a strong sense of duty to continue the entrepreneurial activities of his grandfather and father.

An unassuming, almost shy personality, Konrad Henkel exuded inner strength and calm. Often seen as uncomfortable in public events, he disliked speeches. He was an "active" listener and surrounded himself with competent and trustworthy managers. He closely coordinated the family's business interests with his cousin, Willy Manchot, and later with his son Jürgen, a scion of the Fritz Jr branch of the Henkel family. The unpretentious Henkel understood the need to keep the family members informed about the development of the business; in his branch of the family, which controlled 40 per cent of the ownership, he instituted fortnightly information meetings with his two sisters, who were the only surviving siblings.

When Konrad assumed the business leadership, the Henkel company employed 8,525 workers and produced 500,000 tons of chemical products annually, mainly detergents under the original brand name Persil, as well as newly launched products including Dixan, Pril and Dor. He understood that the company, which had grown from a medium-sized, conservatively managed and very profitable business, would eventually face new challenges. So he started to travel extensively inside Europe, to Japan and especially to the United States. He was intrigued by the growth of Henkel's direct competitor, Procter & Gamble, and studied P&G's business very closely.

Konrad Henkel's background as a chemist kept him focused on the chemical industry. In a markedly application-driven approach, he undertook new diversification efforts, expanding the product range in a gradual, but nevertheless substantial manner. In order to reduce the dependence on the German home market, he also launched a dynamic internationalization process. Throughout this expansion, the predominantly German company also tested other markets. At one stage, it entered the dog food market, but soon gave up that foray, refocusing its main efforts on the core chemical business. From the beginning of his tenure, and long before ecological standards had become popular, Konrad Henkel understood the need to adopt an environmentally friendly philosophy. His practical background as a chemist had taught him that resources were limited.

In the early 1980s, with a stronger appearance of foreign competitors, conditions in the European market started to deteriorate. A worldwide overproduction of detergents led to a price war, and most producers – including Henkel – started losing money for the first time. The only possible strategy for Konrad Henkel was to move forward: growth through acquisitions and continuing diversification. During this period, two major challenges strongly influenced Konrad Henkel's thinking and determined the future impact the Henkel family would have on the company.

Firstly, the continuing growth of the business required financing. During this period of high competition and lower profitability, however, finding money became more and more difficult. Further exacerbating the financial problems, a family member passed away, which resulted in substantial inheritance taxes, and drained both the company and the family.

The Henkel Group had grown substantially and was approaching DM 10 billion in revenues. Konrad Henkel realized that if the family did not want to become an inhibiting element, the role of the family as managers and owners needed to be redefined. After a lengthy reflection process, shared with his cousins and sisters, Konrad Henkel took two sequential decisions that would dramatically alter the role of the family.

The family withdraws from operational management

In 1980, at the age of 65, Konrad Henkel stepped down as the last CEO originating from the Henkel family and handed over the executive control to Professor Sihler, a senior non-family manager. Since Henkel was in good health and could have continued as active leader for a long time, this step surprised most people inside and outside the business. His only motivation appeared to be his desire to redesign the governance structure around the owning family in order to perpetuate the growth of this now very substantial family business, unhindered by issues solely related to the family itself. At the same time, his cousin Jürgen Manchot also stepped down as executive manager. (Members of the "Emmy branch" had previously renounced their right to a management position in the third generation.)

A new nine-member body called the shareholders committee was formed. Five members were directly appointed by the three family branches in accordance with the still-intact distribution of shares as decided by the founder: 40 per cent, 40 per cent and 20 per cent (giving 2, 2 and 1 seats respectively). Four of the nine members were to be highly qualified external non-family business personalities, elected by the family meeting, which included all family shareholders.

With these changes, the right to delegate family members to the shareholders committee replaced the long-standing right of each branch to nominate one family member for a senior management position. According to the new statutes, the shareholders committee had the right to manage the company, and this right had to be delegated to the management board, which included only non-family managers. The committee and the board were scheduled to meet six times a year. Parallel to this new structure, the family agreed unanimously not to sell their shares for about 20 years, or until the year 2000.

The company goes public

To address the needs of the growing business *and* the family, the company was prepared for an initial public offering (IPO) that took place in 1985. The capital was increased in non-voting shares in favour of the family. In order to ensure sufficient liquidity for inheritance taxes, one part was transferred to a heritage pool; a smaller part provided a selling option for family members in need of liquidity.

The public was offered only non-voting shares, and the business obtained fresh money to finance the rapid growth. At the time of the IPO, the Henkel Group had revenues of DM 9.2 billion. By 1996, revenues had ballooned to DM 16.3 billion, both through organic growth and acquisitions, such as Schwarzkopf, another German family business active in cosmetics, and Loctite, a US company active in adhesives.

The next generation

Konrad Henkel continued to influence the development of the Group through his presence in the shareholders committee. He also saw the fourth and the fifth generation of the Henkel family grow to over 60 members. In 1994, knowing that the family shareholder pool agreement would run out in the year 2000, he invited the fourth generation of cousins to start thinking about the future role of the family as shareholders. Over a period of about two years, the fourth- and fifth-generation family members, with no influence from the third generation, held meetings and discussions, partly moderated by outside advisors, with the aim of establishing a long-term plan for the business interests of the family. All options were openly discussed, without taboos:

- Sale of the company, or parts of it
- Minority holdings
- Governance issues.

It quickly became clear that, with the important changes in the eighties having affected the role of the family, the next generations would be more oriented towards creating shareholder value.

In 1996, four years before the first 20-year shareholder agreement was to expire, the fourth- and fifth-generation family members, with the approval of the third generation, produced a new 20-year shareholder agreement. This new agreement, which guaranteed the family ongoing control of the business, had several stipulations:

- Voting shares had to be introduced on the stock exchange
- Every family member has the right to sell some of his or her shares
- The family meeting, including all family shareholders, was given more influence in the acquisitions, company mission, principles and strategy.

Continuing as a family business

The younger generations are committed to remaining responsible majority owners *and* allowing the business to grow. A capital increase in voting shares or a merger is thus excluded. Future growth, therefore, has to be funded through:

- Performance-oriented management
- Holding minority shares in other companies
- Spinning off strategic business units
- Raising additional capital through preferred stocks
- IPOs of subsidiaries.

By the late 1990s, the Henkel family was still growing. Some of its 80 members were living on other continents; very few were living in and around the business headquarters in Düsseldorf. To stay united as a family whose parts share important business interests, the members became part of both formal and informal structures. Until his death in early 1999, Konrad Henkel had been seen as the patriarch of the family who had managed over decades to bring the family together. A large pre-Christmas party in his home was one of the well-established rituals. Further, he had brought the young generation together in an "Information Circle", which still meets three to four times a year. Study groups brought family members to companies and factories of the Henkel Group around the globe. Christoph Henkel, son of Konrad, says, "This is one of the ways the family adds value to the business: showing an interest and demonstrating a long-term commitment to the business is not only important to our employees, but also to our clients, suppliers and stakeholders at large."

In 1999, the Henkel family continues to exercise an important strategic influence on the business. Controlling well over 50 per cent of the voting shares, five family members from the three branches, under the chairmanship of Albrecht Woeste, and aided by four highly respected outside business leaders, regularly meet in the shareholders committee. The family-controlled business generates DM 21 billion in sales, of which only 23 per cent are made up of the original business line (detergents). Other sectors are chemical products (23 per cent), adhesives (22 per cent), cosmetics/toiletries (15 per cent), and hygiene (8 per cent). The Group operates in 70 countries, with Germany generating 23 per cent of total revenue.

Over 57,000 employees are active with 10,000 products. The fourth- and fifth-generation members of the family are firmly committed to the long-term growth of the company. They agree that Henkel can keep growing only if the interests of the business come before those of the family.

Professor Joachim Schwass wrote this article. It is based on interviews with members of the Henkel family, Mr Winkhaus, the non-family CEO of the Group, as well as the presentation of Christoph Henkel on occasion of the 10th Annual World Conference of the Family Business Network in Stockholm, September 1999.

The Zegna Group

IMD Distinguished Family Business Award Winner 2000
By Professor Joachim Schwass

The beginnings of the Ermenegildo Zegna Group as a family business can be traced back to the birth of Angelo Zegna in 1859 in the northwestern part of Italy known as Piedmont. Born the fourth child of a farmer, Angelo worked as a watchmaker when he later became a weaver, which was the then most common industry in this isolated and impoverished mountainous area. Records traced back to the thirteenth century already indicate a flourishing activity of wool making initiated by shepherds around the town of Biella. A Guild of Wool Makers had established norms for weaving and dyeing wool. In the beginning of the nineteenth century, water-powered mechanical looms and spinning machines were introduced into the area which provided both plentiful hydraulic and human resources. This was the start of the industrial revolution for Northern Italy.

At the age of 40, Angelo Zegna operated a textile manufacturing plant, with about 15 looms, which was destroyed by a fire. In 1907 he rebuilt it in the small town of Trivero. Amongst his ten children, it was his last-born son in 1892, Ermenegildo, who would have the strongest impact on what would eventually become one of the largest and most dynamic Italian family businesses.

Angelo, being busy building the small spinning plant, confided the education of his son Ermenegildo at the age of six to the local parish priest. Accompanying the priest on his rounds exposed the young child to both sad and joyous rites: witnessing births and deaths in this isolated mountain village opened his eyes to the hardship of its inhabitants. This was a time of poverty, hard work also for children as shepherds or in the small textile factories. Many inhabitants emigrated trying to find a better life elsewhere. Ermenegildo, described as a bright, curious and intelligent child also joined his brothers in his father's factory. After having served in World War I he returned to nearby Biella and completed technical studies at the professional textile institute. In 1923, Angelo Zegna, the founder and entrepreneur, passed away. Ermenegildo soon emerged as the next leader of the family business. Having worked closely with his father he understood the business very well. But Ermenegildo had a very different concept of an entrepreneur: he felt the need for a more humane approach to leadership and he was convinced that technological advances would be the vehicles allowing him to implement a more modern and social vision.

Having observed the higher quality of English textiles, he travelled and studied what he felt were vastly better manufacturing processes. He became driven by the deep-seated desire to become better than his English competitors. In 1930, the family firm started producing high-quality textiles using the latest imported English spinning machines. Most unusual for this industry, the name Ermenegildo Zegna became a trademark applied to the fine fabrics that were supplied to designers and private customers. Rich and creative designs were produced – some of which are still used today.

By the end of the 1930s, the company employed 1,000 workers. In 1942, the company was split into Ermenegildo Zegna and Sons, continuing the same process of wool production, and a new establishment under the control of Mario, one of his brothers. Ermenegildo now had control over the business, which had flourished under his leadership. A hard worker, described as a calm and secure person, he had already then created an exceptional legacy. Beginning in 1932, he had started building hospitals, hotels, sports facilities and a professional training school. The factories were light and airy, creating a pleasant working environment. He built a beautiful scenic road – the Panoramica Zegna – linking one village to the next. His project comprised the reforesting of mountain slopes with 500,000 conifers, rhododendrons and hydrangeas. The 65-kilometre-long road was to bring new life to the mountains above Trivero. Ermenegildo's children and grandchildren will expand this extraordinary environmental project.

The business continued to flourish as workers were highly motivated to work for this socially advanced company and as Ermenegildo continued to excel as an outstanding leader and entrepreneur. Always impeccably dressed, he could be seen observing the dress codes of his countrymen on all sorts of occasions. He undertook his own market research, always wanting to be at the forefront of innovation and best quality supplies. He invited many tailors to visit the factory. While the English fabric manufacturers imposed a 50-metre-length minimum order size per fabric, which many tailors disliked as it led to systematic overstocking, Ermenegildo offered a more flexible order and delivery condition based on the actual fabric requirement per suit. An enthusiastic traveller, already in 1938 the first Ermenegildo Zegna fabrics were imported into the United States and initially sold to immigrant Italian tailors who remembered the brand. Zegna was the first branded product to be advertised on Italian trains. During World War II, a time of scarcity, the already legendary high-quality market perception of Zegna fabrics was reinforced by the fact that many tailors used previously worn fabrics by just reversing them. The fabrics were already exported to over 40 countries, which provided the necessary foreign currencies needed to finance the purchase of the finest Australian wool as raw material.

The enormous achievements of Ermenegildo Zegna, as an early social entrepreneur, are described by his younger son Angelo Zegna in the following words:

I see four important forces, which influenced my father's life:

- Firstly, he was born into the right environment which could foster his entrepreneurial behaviour: a cluster of many competitors in a physically constrained, small area

- Secondly, he was intensely driven by the vision to beat the English competitors by offering fabrics with Italian design creativity at unsurpassed quality levels
- Thirdly, an extraordinary open mind, especially in regards to the social welfare and giving back to the workers
- Lastly, his closeness to nature understanding that resources are limited and must be protected. He was an ecologist well before the word existed!

Angelo, born 1924, and his brother Aldo, born in 1920, both joined their father's business very early on in their lives. As children, they spent each day after school and at least half of each school holiday working in the factory. The boys were supervised by a nanny who spoke German with them. Learning English and French and travelling at an early age were high on the list of educational priorities. But first and foremost Ermenegildo wanted his sons to share his love for wool and fabrics, for the highest quality combined with beautiful designs.

The father was reported to be strict but not severe, allowing his sons time for sports and diversions.

Aldo, the elder son, studied engineering, while Angelo undertook studies in economics and commerce. This would be the functional separation, which the brothers would observe during their working careers.

After the difficulties of World War II, the father, in close cooperation with his sons, concentrated on modernizing the manufacturing plants. By 1955, Ermenegildo Zegna and Sons employed 1,400 workers. The focus of attention gradually shifted to the creation of new designs and styles. But essentially until the death of Ermenegildo in 1966, at the age of 74, the firm was a manufacturer of fabrics for men's clothing, building on its spinning roots. The sons Aldo and Angelo, who were firmly in control of all operations, had observed that their traditional clients, the tailors of men's suits, gradually disappeared. This market shift now seemed to open up new opportunities for them, and in an opportunistic yet strategic move they decided to expand their business activities to include the manufacture of ready-made suits on an industrial base. They also believed that high-quality suits made industrially would make suits more accessible to the broader population. While traditionally suits were worn on Sundays, after the war, suits became increasingly commonplace also in workplaces and offices. Angelo, with his commercial background, took on this exciting new challenge and "Zegna Confection" was launched in 1968 with a new plant in Novara, northern Italy. Being able to capitalize on an already well-known brand for their fabrics and now for their ready-made suits gave this new business enormous credibility and almost instant success. While Aldo looked after the traditional fabric-making activities, Angelo focused his energy on this new division. Convinced of their successful business model in Italy, they started to look for markets outside Italy as an expansion and risk diversification strategy. They focused on Spain as a country with many cultural and structural similarities with Italy and launched their first foreign plant for ready-made suits in 1973. Their assessments were proven right: the first year this new operation broke even, and it turned a profit in the second year. The expansion pattern seemed to be clear for the brothers, and in 1975 they opened the second foreign plant in Greece. But, as Angelo says, this proved to be a mistake:

We believed that Greece with its very low labour cost would provide similar structures and advantages as Spain. But we hit many problems, the main one being that during harvest times the women working in the factory just walked out and we literally had no workers for weeks! We realized that this just would not work and that we had to be realistic and cut our losses. After two years we closed the operations.

Meanwhile, the growing demand on the Italian production had created bottlenecks, which were further exacerbated by an increasingly unreliable working environment riddled by strikes. It became ever more difficult to work and plan in this unpredictable economic scenery. The Zegnas looked then at the Italian part of Switzerland as a point of production. The Canton of Ticino, less than an hour's drive from Milan, promised a stable working environment with considerably lower taxes and surprisingly, lower manufacturing costs thanks to flexible cross-border workers resources. In 1977, the Zegnas opened a plant for men's suits in the southern part of the Canton of Ticino.

This now provided them with a stable, reliable and highest quality manufacturing facility for men's suits. It was on this platform that the next strategic expansion step took place: building on their expertise in ready-to-wear men's suits, they now also offered made-to-measure men's suits. Aldo and Angelo Zegna had observed the gradual disappearance of individual tailors during and after the war and made-to-measure suits became in most countries an expensive luxury.

But the brothers had a deep understanding of the meaning of perfectly adapted clothes to the differing shapes of the human body; even the best-manufactured ready-to-wear suit could never reach that perfection.

Now, through their plant in Switzerland and an ingenious setting up of measuring devices and systems, they could offer the perfection of a made-to-measure suit through selected key distributors around the world at a price not much different to a good ready-to-wear suit. Over the years, new computer aided design and manufacturing techniques were introduced. Today, the Zegna family business employs over 800 workers in the Italian area of Switzerland alone, demonstrating the success of this new market offering.

While the 1960s and 1970s proved to be decades of growth for many European countries, the success and dynamic entrepreneurial expansion of the Zegna business has to be sought in the family's leadership. Aldo and Angelo Zegna learned all about business by working closely with their father until their early forties. Ermenegildo Zegna was the modern social entrepreneur, a hard worker striving for perfection, uncompromised quality and closeness to the customer. Yet he was also close to nature, understanding the need for balance in all his undertakings. Often self-effacing, he frequently delegated social and formal responsibilities to his sons. After he had passed away, the sons assumed his legacy and adapted it to the modern world. They became entrepreneurs in their own right and took the family business to new strategic levels, but by always building on the achieved, on the tradition. They shared ownership equally. The two brothers drew enormous energy from the close team that they formed. Aldo, with his engineering background, was the more cautious thinker, while his younger brother Angelo, with his commercial background was more intuitive and innovation driven. Marco Vitale, a professor and consultant, who is today a member of the board of the Zegna Group, was initially brought in as a business process consultant in the 1970s. Having observed the interaction between the two brothers over decades, he commented:

> To an outsider, it seemed like there was always conflict between Aldo and Angelo. There were loud discussions and disagreements. But they were always on a professional base – they had the deepest personal respect for each other and of course they were very close. But these frequent discussions really allowed them to analyze a given problem from all angles, be creative, intuitive, rational and finally come up with a well thought out, down-to-earth solution. That close, familiar yet professional relationship was the backbone of their successful, third generation leadership.

Meanwhile, the fourth generation of Zegnas was growing up. Aldo had four children born between 1950 and 1961; Angelo also had four children born between 1955 and 1965. As their father Ermenegildo had done with them, so Aldo and Angelo brought up their children with an outlook on the modern world, travelling, learning languages and studying abroad, but always recognizing the roots of the family firm that had started in Trivero. Aldo had maintained his residence in his hometown, close to the fabric-making plant. Angelo had moved closer to the suit-making plant in Ticino. The fourth generation understood the importance of the roots in Trivero and the outstanding social achievements of their grandfather.

Gildo Zegna, son of Angelo, says:

> For my cousin Paolo and myself it was always natural to join the family business. The business carries the name of the family, so somehow it was all part of us. But we also understood that there were rules of behavior if indeed we did enter the business: Education, languages, university degrees and outside work experience.

Paolo, born 1956 as son of Aldo, and Gildo, born 1955 as son of Angelo, emerged as the natural next-generation leaders. Paolo graduated in business studies at the University of Geneva and worked in Spain and Australia for several years. Gildo graduated at the University of London and gained a BA from the Harvard Business School before working for Bloomingdale's as a buyer. He then joined Zegna in the US.

As their fathers had done, they worked their way up in different functions and it was in 1998, when they were both in their forties that they became joint CEOs with Angelo and Aldo giving up their executive responsibilities and moving to the board. This was not always an easy time for the two generations to work together. Both Gildo and Paolo aspired to more managerial control and freedom earlier on. Marco Vitale, the outsider who had joined the board, played a crucial role in facilitating the succession process. He says:

> I was the facilitator between the generations. When discussions became difficult, I urged the younger ones to take courage and speak up. Indeed it was sometimes intimidating to follow and wanting to add something to the intensive and heated discussions between Angelo and Aldo. But I defended Gildo and Paolo when I felt they were right and over time the situation became more balanced. As an outsider, I could take some of the emotions out of the discussion and bring them to a rational base.

Meanwhile, the business had gone from strength to strength with the opening up of new markets and manufacturing plants. In 1999, the Zegna Group had eight manufacturing plants in Italy, two in Spain, three in Switzerland, one in Mexico and one in Turkey. The range of manufactured products covered fabrics, suits, ties, knitwear, shirts, accessories and sportswear. But the family showed yet another sign of entrepreneurial growth by moving into retailing. Over decades, the business had been built on the strength of the brand name, manufacturing and supplying highest-quality products to European, Asian and American markets through Zegna-owned import companies, carefully selecting the best distributors and investing in brand building. But the family felt that Ermenegildo Zegna's legacy was to be as close as possible to the consumer. And by doing that they would better understand consumer needs and they could better transmit their vision of quality. Gildo explains the cornerstones of the Zegna vision: "We call it the Zegna Box with its four corners: quality, modernity, masculinity, naturalness. Whatever we do under the Zegna brand, it has to fit into the box."

In 1980, Zegna opened the first fully owned retail store in Paris. It took five years before they opened the next store in Milan. After several years of trial and error, the family successfully learned yet again how another business functions. Other fourth-generation family members were involved in launching Zegna into retailing: Paolo's younger brother Andrea works as an architect. Gildo's younger sisters Anna and Benedetta work in communication and training. The entire family is drawn into this energizing new strategic direction for the group. Dozens of new retail stores are opened around the world. If break-even is not achieved within three years, they are unconditionally closed. Anna Zegna says: "We are realistic and not concerned about possibly losing face: if a new store does not work, we close it!" In the year 2000, there were over 300 Zegna stores around the world, one third fully owned and the rest under franchise.

The year 2000 was a successful milestone: group sales were around US$600 million with pretax profits of 12 per cent of sales in 1999. Total assets have more than doubled in the 1996–99 period. The group is debt-free. Zegna is widely considered the world leader in fine men's clothing, with a market share of 30 per cent and a yearly output of over 2 million metres of fabric, 350,000 suits, 1 million sportswear items and 1.5 million ties. The group employs 4,500 workers worldwide, of which 1,500 are in Italy. Sales by area are: the Americas: 40 per cent, Europe: 40 per cent and Asia: 20 per cent.

But the year 2000 also brought the passing away of Aldo Zegna. His brother Angelo, as president, continues to keep an alert eye on the fortunes of the business which is now firmly in the hands of the fourth generation. Ownership continues to be equally divided between the two branches. It is possible for a family member to sell shares to another family member, but at a predetermined formula with a heavy discount. But the family ties appear to be as strong in this generation as in the previous one. The fourth generation has introduced an astonishing degree of financial transparency – but as Marco Vitale says, only after very long discussions with their fathers. Today, this not only enables the two co-CEOs to motivate their employees around the world, but it also provides responsible and transparent reporting back to the board and the owners. The board is made up of Angelo, three members of the fourth generation and the trusted outsider Marco Vitale.

The co-CEOs state that they are running the business as if it were a public corporation. Asked if they would consider selling, the reply was instinctively negative: "At least not in this generation!" They are aggressively pursuing a dynamic expansion strategy on several fronts:

- The launch of a new, softer sports range initially in the United States, under the name of Zegna Sport
- Exploring opportunities in the market for women's clothing through the acquisition of the Agnona business in Italy
- A new joint venture with Armani to manufacture men's clothing in newly bought factories of the joint venture under the Armani collection brand.

The Zegna Group is a totally integrated business, controlling the entire value chain from raw materials right through to the final sale of a finished product to the customer. It is a successful business which has built on traditions and values as defined by earlier generations but which each generation has successfully redefined and adapted to the changed world. Anna Zegna talks about the role of a family business:

> For the Zegnas it all started with a social commitment to the small community and the people of Trivero. We pass these values on to our children from generation to generation and it is the duty of the family to bring these values to the company. Thus the family business is a point of reference of values. Governments are faceless today; they can no longer provide guidance on values.

The young leaders of the family business, Gildo and Paolo, define the important values for them and the family as:

- Self-respect
- Discipline
- Hard work
- Honesty
- Trust.

The respect for the roots of the Zegna family is being kept alive also by the fourth generation: building on Ermenegildo's Panoramica road in Trivero, in 1993 the Oasi Zegna was launched as a 100-square-kilometre reserve of meadows and forest. Fourth-generation Laura Zegna oversees this first Italian example of environmental patronage. Its mission is to promote environmental education and to encourage direct contact with nature through sport and soft tourism.

The guiding principles of the family were explained in the following words by Aldo Zegna addressing the key employees at a company convention in Venice in June 1999:

> The virtues of our father Ermenegildo did not only include intelligence and great vision but also perseverance, dedication and coherence, and this is the legacy that Angelo and I received which has fueled and guided our activity. Being able to predict the future, having intuition, working courageously with persistence as well as having sensitivity for social causes are the messages, which I give you now when our working life is about to close. This message has been received

by our children in their capable and confident hands to work as intended. The future is in God's hands, but the premises for success are there. Continue working as you have been doing with enthusiasm, clear ideas, dedication and you cannot fail to be successful.

Professor Joachim Schwass wrote this article, based on interviews with Zegna family members and employees and publications by Piero Chiara and the Zegna Group

The Murugappa Group

IMD Distinguished Family Business Award Winner 2001
By Professor John L. Ward, Wild Group Professor of Family Business, IMD, and Co-Director of the Center for Family Enterprises

2001 IMD Award Winners, The Murugappa Group, have drawn upon their business acumen, heritage and faith in the family system to help them successfully adapt to change.

The Murugappa Group, headquartered in Chennai (Madras), India, has grown from humble beginnings to become a very important conglomerate. The company started as the dream of a driven entrepreneur in Burma in the early 1900s. Today it boasts revenues of US$850 million and employs 22,500 people in its 27 business units. The company is presently undergoing a major change, as it restructures its family governance system. It realizes that change is necessary if they want to continue to compete in the world marketplace. Though adaptation is not always easy, the Murugappas find strength through their heritage and values.

An entrepreneurial spirit

The family traces its business history to 1760 when the great-great-great-grandfather of the founder was active in trading and money lending. He had five sons who each, separately, built successful businesses that, in later generations, led to leadership in several industries in India. The family came from a long line of members of the Chettiar sub-clan of the Vaisyas caste-merchants and professionals with business interests primarily in Burma, Malaysia, Sri Lanka and Vietnam, known for their scrupulous honesty, trustworthiness, cleverness in trade and proficiency in money matters.

The Group's founder was Dewan Bahadur Arunachalam Murugappa Murugappa Chettiar (known as Dewan Bahadur), the youngest of three sons, born in 1884. Following Indian tradition, the majority control of his deceased father's entire estate went to the eldest son, with Dewan Bahadur receiving virtually nothing for all his work. The unfairness of this policy spurred him to divide his estate equally among his three sons – Murugappa, Vellayan and AMM. He did this while they were young men and while he was still alive to give them the freedom and the opportunity to be a family energetically pursuing business together. He also encouraged free speech among his sons until a decision was taken; then the courtesies due to an elder had to be honoured. This, too, varied from the norm in society at the time where respect for the elder was paramount.

All three of Dewan Bahadur's sons shared their father's venturesome business spirit and complemented each other in their managerial styles. Murugappa was marketing and external relations-oriented; Vellayan was finance-oriented; and AMM was operations-oriented, with a focus on details.

In the early 1930s, Dewan Bahadur and his sons made several decisions that were critical to their later success. At a time when 70 per cent of Chettiar wealth was in Burma, they repatriated much of their monies to India so that the Great Depression, World War II and Burmese national movements didn't bankrupt the family; they had an insight that India was on the verge of industrialization; and they decided to take the family's first steps into major industry.

With the repatriated funds, they established a sandpaper plant (the beginning of today's US$65 million abrasives business called CUMI); they purchased a steel safe manufacturing company; they started an insurance company; and they bought a rubber plantation. The Murugappa Group was born.

In 1931, Dewan Bahadur's eldest son, Murugappa, visited the US for the International Chambers of Commerce Convention. This trip broadened the family's view of possibilities for making money and expanding the company.

When Murugappa returned from the US, he kept an eye out for a business opportunity he could set up and lead in India. When he heard from an acquaintance that there was market demand in India for a quality manufacturer of steel security furniture such as safes, cashboxes and filing cabinets, he moved forward with family support, commencing production in 1940.

A much larger foray, conceived during the same time period, was to enter the business of making abrasives, a product used by manufacturers to sand, sharpen and smooth equipment, materials, components and end products. The family's rationale was that if world war broke out, the volume and variety of goods imported on British ships would decrease; thus local manufacturing would expand with the new opportunity. The family cleverly negotiated to buy, dismantle, ship and install an abrasives plant from the American Midwest to its location in India. The plant was operational in 1942.

About a decade later, AMM made contact with the three largest abrasives companies in the world – to seek a joint venture for access to new technologies. When all three were disinterested or very slow to respond, he contacted and struck a deal with Carborundum USA and Universal of UK. Before anything official was signed, the largest company in the field made overtures and showed interest. Since the family had given its word to the British company, they would not go back on it to negotiate with one of their larger, first-choice firms. This was the first of many successful joint venture arrangements (since 1952 named Carborundum Universal of Madras, India, or CUMI).

After India gained independence in 1947, the Murugappa family was among the first in India to form a joint venture. With introductions by Sir A. Ramaswami Mudaliar, some experience in steel manufacturing of safes and with a vision for bicycles in India, Tube Investments of India (TII) was formed in 1949. TII began as a bicycle assembly firm representing the English Hercules brand in India. The English partner began with a 43 per cent interest. Over time, TII grew, integrated into most all components, and diversified into steel tubes for furniture, industry and other applications. Hercules became the number one bicycle company in India.

The British partner eventually departed the industry, turned the Hercules, BSA and Philips brand over to the Murugappas and divested its ownership position.

One of the patterns in the Group's development is that their foreign partners lose interest in the Indian venture due to acquisition, management or strategy changes and sell back their shares to the family at a better than fair price because of the trusting relationship they had built. This happened, for example, with CUMI in 1982 when its UK parent sold back its shares. CUMI, now publicly traded, is 43 per cent controlled by the family.

Adaptation and growth

In India's government-regulated economy, the Murugappa Group found it necessary to adapt in order to prosper. In the 1980s, Indian law prohibited formation of a business group, so the family followed the system of cross-holding controlling shares among separate public companies. Recently, that law has changed, and the family is restructuring again to become a holding company.

Because of government regulation in the past, it was difficult to obtain licences for new businesses. Between 1964 and 1980, the Group applied for 17 licences. Out of the 17 licence applications, one was granted and the other 16 were not. The Group decided not to pursue these because of their values. Consequently, to grow, they sought acquisition of ailing units to turn around. In the last 20 years, 17 additional companies have been acquired.

The most well-publicized acquisition occurred in 1981 with the purchase of Madras-based EID Parry – a huge, decrepit yet symbolic business that the Group had been interested in since 1958. Parry, the second oldest commercial name in India, included fertilizers, pesticides, confectionery and also sugar mills. For years, EID Parry's creditors were asking the Group to take over its management, given the Group's management reputation and acumen. The family repeatedly turned down the overtures, responding that without control EID Parry wasn't in the family interests. Eventually, the creditors relented and the family gained control of the publicly traded company. The agreement made headlines because it showed the Group's commitment to invest in what many in India felt was a risky venture, but what they saw as an opportunity to grow. EID Parry is now a business with US$265 million in sales and is 41 percent family-owned.

With EID Parry came a 7 per cent holding in a joint venture fertilizer company, CoRomendel Fertilizers Ltd Chevron and IMC Global, partnered in the fertilizer growth area then later sold out. EID Parry developed a unique organic pesticide from indigenous neem seeds that is often acclaimed to be the best in the world. EID Parry is also in the sanitary ware business. However, not all businesses have been a success. For example, the Group has divested a cement company, sold its electronics business and faced difficulties with its long-held construction company.

Business and philanthropy

Today the Group includes seven substantial business units comprising 27 companies in a variety of industries: CUMI, TII, CoRomendel, Parry Agro, EID Parry, CIFCO and the only private company, Ambadi Estates, holder of some of the plantations. TII now has four significant lines: bicycles, chains, industrial tubes and roll forming. CUMI is a full line, vertically integrated abrasives company and CoRomendel is a very profitable fertilizer business. With Ambadi and Parry Agro, the Group remains active in rubber, tea and coffee plantations. EID Parry includes an assortment of businesses including fertilizers, sugar mills, pesticides and sanitary ware. The Group is in the food industry with Parrys Confectionery Ltd. CIFCO is in the financial services of brokerage, vehicle finance, insurance and mutual funds.

The Murugappa Group and family also continue to build on the example of philanthropy initiated by Dewan Bahadur. His decision to set aside a major portion of his wealth for charitable causes, starting in 1924 when he built a hospital in his home village, commenced a tradition of helping, guiding and supporting others in communities in which the companies do business. The family's trust, the AMM Foundation, is sustained by a fixed percentage of annual business profits and family contributions. To date it has built and nurtured four high schools of 8,000 students, a polytechnic institute of 1,000 students, four no-fee hospitals and a rural research centre. The rural research centre focuses its activities on developing such things as protein-efficient algae, natural dyes, organic farming and technologies for the rural and urban poor. Although by custom, the sisters and wives of the Murugappa men do not work in the businesses, they are the major sources of leadership and guidance in the family's foundation and the institutions it supports.

Family ties

While success seems to overflow for the Murugappas, the family and business have also been shaped by trauma and loss. Tragedy first struck in late 1945 at the end of World War II. Middle son Vellayan, age 40, was assassinated while in Burma as part of a formal delegation gauging the safety of Indian civilians returning to the newly communist country. From then on, his two brothers functioned in the business roles as "Mr Outside" (Murugappa) and "Mr Inside" (AMM), under the overall leadership of the elder – their father until his death in 1949, Murugappa until his death in 1965 and AMM until his death in 1999.

Beginning in the late 1950s, the third-generation sons entered the business. They successfully avoided a common family business trap of an enterprise slumping after the founder's generation. This was due to their elders' concerted focus on developing the talents of the younger members as professionals through academic training, international experience, at least two years' work outside of the family business and finally employment at a mid-level in the Group's companies, rising one step at a time. Up through the mid-1990s, each of the six male family members in the third generation rose to become managing director of one or more of the business units.

MV, first son of Vellayan and the oldest of his generation, set the pace with higher education at a college. While working at businesses within the Group, MV was encouraged by his uncle AMM, the chairman, to play roles in the business world beyond the family, including positions on boards, associations and delegations. He held managing director or joint managing director positions at Carborundum, later CUMI, TII and CoRomendel until his death in 1996.

Muthiah, second son of Vellayan, was adopted as a teen by his uncle Murugappa who had no male heirs. He held several positions with the family firms, including Ambadi Estates where he became a leading authority on planting in southern India. He worked at CoRomendel Engineering and was the managing director of CUMI when he died suddenly in 1979 at age 49.

Murugappan, the third son of Vellayan trained as a civil engineer in England and used his expertise to successfully scout unique new lines of industrial products to manufacture and sell in India. He took over the managing director position of CUMI when Muthiah died and continues as chairman of CUMI to this day. Since 1999, he has been the family elder, but decided against the leadership of the business, deferring to his younger brother, Subbiah.

Subbiah, the youngest son of Vellayan, has his college degree from the University of Aston in England. He is credited with a major role in turning ailing EID Parry into a successful business in the 1980s, serving as vice-chairman and managing director. He also had leadership positions at TI Cycles, as the chairman of the Murugappa Group and the Executive chairman of EID Parry. In 1996 he was appointed Group CEO.

Muru, the oldest son of AMM, studied mechanical engineering in England, followed by on-the-job training at Tube Investments Group UK. He worked at, then headed up CoRomendel Engineering, the family's construction business. He died in 1995 at age 55.

Algy is the second son of AMM. After schooling in Lawrence at Ooty and gaining his degree in commerce in India, he went to Britain as a management trainee with TI. He started his work experience at TI Cycles and subsequently moved up to number two to Muthiah in the plantation business. He was instrumental in starting up the Cholamandalam financial services business. Currently he is vice-chairman of the Murugappa Group and chairman of Cholamandalam.

Since the late 1970s, six of seven sons in the fourth generation have also joined the Group, making contributions in the business units at all levels including managing director. All men of the same generation and age who work in the family business receive equal compensation and perks, regardless of title, position, contribution or level of responsibility within the organization. To enhance individual and Group success, informal mentoring among the family members takes place with older, more experienced and/or accomplished members guiding, assisting and supporting younger, less experienced members. As for inheritance, equal thirds of the family's business shares – following the three branches of the family emanating from the three sons of Dewan Bahadur – are divided and entrusted to the males in each generation, whether they work in the business or not.

Transitions

An important transition in organization occurred in 1985 when the Group hired for the first time a management consultant, AD Little, to look at issues of structure and succession. This effort resulted in a leadership succession plan in which senior members of the family of the third generation filled the positions of business unit managing directors, COO and CEO until each retired at 65, with the selection process based on merit as well as seniority.

After India signed the World Trade Organization agreement around 1995, the family saw opportunities, including new export-oriented activities. Because of this, they realized the necessity of making speedier business portfolio decisions than was presently possible due to individual family members being emotionally involved in separate business units. In this environment, even when everyone wanted to make a positive business decision for the Group as a whole, it could not be made with the speed and nimbleness necessary in the faster pace of the new global economy.

Despite this realization, nothing changed until 1996 when Muru and MV both died at early ages. These tragic events acted as a wake-up call. The family elder, AMM, urged a restructuring to improve the future of the business by relying less on family members for the day-to-day management of the business units as managing directors. Leadership of this task fell to AMM until his death in 1999, then to his nephew Murugappan who continues as family elder today, and to Subbiah, appointed Group CEO in 1996.

The goal of the restructuring was to introduce change without disrupting performance in an atmosphere of openness and support. The family leaders sought the help of an esteemed Indian colleague to help facilitate discussions of change among family members. Several insights about the Murugappa Group's reorganization surfaced, which included the need:

1. To be more of a Group rather than a collection of separate entities
2. To be more flexible in the makeup of the portfolio of businesses
3. To have less emotional attachment by individuals to their businesses
4. To shift away from family-led units to non-family-led units
5. To mentor the non-family managing directors for the long-term view.

Facilitating change

To facilitate the change process, the family members on the board committed one to two days a month for almost two years. This resulted in establishing a holding company-like board with the intention of becoming an actual holding company in the future. In 1999, the Murugappa Group created the new governance structure. They changed the leadership of the individual business units from family members to professional managers and the family members moved to board positions on the newly formed nine-member Murugappa Corporate Board (MCB). This holding company-like board includes as directors five family members (two from the third generation and three from the fourth generation), three independent members and the Group CFO. The independent board members recognized the importance of their participation in the transition of the company and wanted to work with the Murugappa family members because of their exceptional experience, humility and a willingness to listen. They also wanted to demonstrate the success of the holding company model for family business and to ensure the family business as an important force in the economy of India.

The new structure was innovative for the business and for India. At once, it allowed family members on the board to focus on strategic areas across businesses for the benefit of the entire organization. Each family member on the MCB serves as a full-time director with three assigned responsibilities. One is for a function across all business units, another is to serve as mentor/overseer for one or more businesses he has typically never led before, and the third is to guide younger family members for future governance roles.

One of the benefits of this arrangement has been the creation of knowledge transfer and technology synergies among the Group's businesses. The move harnessed the substantial business experience and resourcefulness of the family members for the good of the overall company, not just a business unit, and also brought a new perspective from the independent board members.

The family members on the board have noticed great value in the restructuring, although it is not without personal challenges because they are being stretched to perform in areas new to them with different people, operations and situations.

The changes made in the management and leadership of the business were also noticed by workers, family and community. The family board members are aware that they are serving as role models of the structural change, especially in bringing along other constituent groups that need to make adjustments to the new arrangement. The new governing structures caused a shift in decision making to one that is more collaborative – a counter to Indian norms and values of the traditional leadership role of elders in the family.

Future focus

As the business moves from family-operated to family-governed, formalizing the family's business approach is being discussed within the family and among the MCB members. The family has taken steps towards articulating what they stand for by developing their *corporate values and beliefs*. These are listed prominently on their corporate materials, website, and *bill of rights* and *responsibilities for family member owners*, all of which can be amended by family consensus but not by vote. The development of a family constitution is seen as the next important step, but the form the family constitution takes – whether it should be a formal written document or an understanding by custom and practice – is under discussion. Independent directors are trying to get the family to formalize procedures because the businesses' complexity demands it.

Family and independent directors of the board realize that the future role of family members in the business is evolving. They are aware that family members in future generations will have more choices in terms of profession than in the past and may opt out of the business. Those who enter the business need education, development and training to be future leaders in the family business at the governing level, although they will not be managing directors of units.

Up until April 2001, the MCB was headed by a family member, Subbiah. At that time, he stepped aside and independent board member NS Raghavan took over as the MCB's first independent non-family executive chairman on an interim basis. The reasons for this change were to create an environment that encourages creativity and fuels growth and to make decision making even more rational and less personal. The board is proceeding slowly to find a permanent non-family MCB chairman, preferring to wait for a person who is just right for the position.

In the last decade, the Group has looked at its portfolio of businesses with an eye towards future growth. Although many of the Group's long-term companies are in low-margin, old economy manufacturing, there has been a continued focus on investing in and maximizing research for the good of the business. Several of the business units have launched products developed as a direct result of its proprietary research investments that could have global markets. The value of supporting research for product innovation is a priority.

The company also seeks to balance and reduce its portfolio of companies to the six business areas it knows well and in which it holds leadership positions. The Group plans to shift reliance away from low but steady growth manufacturing to opportunities in the high growth financial services sector through its business unit,

CIFCO, where it has managerial and financial capability. The Group is increasing exports and is exploring entirely new opportunities in industries that are global employing the highly talented yet cost-effective Indian workforce. One such endeavour under development is information technology enabled products.

For the Murugappa Group family business leaders, the last three years have been times of great structural changes, shifts in thinking and adaptation, all the while managing a major spectrum of successful businesses and opportunities in a marketplace that is increasingly fast-paced and global. Sustaining them through these substantial efforts in meeting success in the future have been the valuable lessons of their family's heritage. Throughout the generations, family members in the business have used situations presented to them as springboards from which to creatively adjust, flex and move forward for the good of family and community. They have anticipated change, shown a willingness to adapt and to take risks. As fourth-generation Murugu reflected when he accepted, on behalf of his family, the IMD Distinguished Family Business Award in October 2001 in Rome:

> We consider ourselves custodians to a heritage and trustees to a tradition, both built on togetherness, trust, mutual respect, ethical values and above all dignity, independence and discipline. As the scope and magnitude of the family and business leadership changes, we are preparing ourselves for the great challenges ahead. This award reinforces our faith in family and also in our ability to build business and public institutions.

Samuel C. Johnson Family Enterprises

IMD Distinguished Family Business Award Winner 2002
By Professor Joachim Schwass, Professor of Family Business, IMD, and Director, The IMD-Lombard Odier Darier Hentsch Family Business Center

"We should worry not about whether we have lived up to the expectations of our fathers ... but whether we, as fathers, live up to the expectations of our children."

Sam Johnson

The founder of what is today the Samuel C. Johnson Family Enterprises was Samuel Curtis Johnson (1833–1919). In his early working years, Johnson was employed at the Racine Hardware Company, where he sold parquet floors. In 1886, he acquired the parquet flooring business, which in its first year generated a profit of US$268.27.

Recognizing people's need to treat wooden floors, Johnson developed a wax product from beeswax and other components that he mixed in a bathtub. In 1888 he introduced Johnson Prepared Wax and bought his first national advertising in the *Saturday Evening Post*. By the turn of the century, wax sales were larger than the revenues from selling parquet floors, so Johnson discontinued the sales of parquet. As the company's wax products gained wide acceptance, Johnson exported them to Britain and even as far as Australia, and the number of employees ballooned to over 100. By 1900, Johnson Wax was at the forefront in human resources policies, offering paid vacations to the employees. In 1917, it introduced a profit-sharing plan that gave employees 25 per cent of the company's earnings.

In 1919, Samuel C. Johnson died, and his son, Herbert Fisk Johnson (1868–1928) took over. Herbert's sister, Jessie, neither worked in the business nor inherited ownership. Herbert, who had joined the business at 20, working closely with his father, became an equal partner in 1906, at which time the company became SC Johnson & Son. On Samuel's death in 1919, Herbert, then 51, became president. More technical than his father, Herbert's research-orientation led to a number of new cleaning and treating products, which earned him a reputation as the "real business builder" through diversification. In 1926, Herbert, who shared his father's strong sense of social responsibility, established a 40-hour workweek, calling his approach "enlightened selfishness". In 1927, on occasion of the Christmas Profit Sharing, Herbert gave a widely respected speech that still serves as a philosophical guide for current generations: "The goodwill of the people is the only enduring thing in any business. It is the sole substance ... the rest is shadow!"

In 1928, Herbert unexpectedly died at age 59 and left the family business devoid of any will or succession plan. His son, Herbert Fisk (HF) Johnson Jr (1899–1978), assumed management control – he was 28. It took a decade to clarify ownership with Henrietta, HF's younger sister, who eventually received one third of the shares. This protracted legal battle caused HF to state that he was "never going to let that happen to [his] son", and in his will he subsequently designated his son, Sam, as his successor.

HF led the 500-strong company through the Great Depression with no layoffs. He is widely seen as the creator of international growth and the progenitor of new manufacturing technologies. HF was, in fact, the company's first chemist. On the personal side, besides the relatively early loss of his father, he also suffered the death of his four-year-old daughter and a subsequent divorce from his first wife, who suffered from alcoholism. The other two children, Karen and Sam, moved between their father in the Midwest and their mother in New York.

After the Depression years, HF started to worry about the supply of the key ingredient in the company's wax products, which comes from the carnauba palm in the Brazilian rain forest. His background as a chemist had raised his awareness of the importance not only of the manufacturing technology, but also about the nature of the raw materials used in production. Believing strongly in product quality he launched the "Product Plus" concept: every new Johnson product had to have a distinct advantage over everything else on the market, or it had to be new and unique enough to outstrip the competition.

In 1935, HF bought an amphibious plane and led a 22,000-mile expedition from Milwaukee to the Brazilian rain forest to study the carnauba palm tree. The trip, which received broad press coverage, was described by *Time* magazine as "Johnson's search for the 'tree of life'". The expedition had a strong, favourable impact on the 36-year-old HF. He returned invigorated and full of new visions for the business. In 1936, he invited Frank Lloyd Wright to design the new company headquarters in Racine, Wisconsin. He also wrote a book about his Brazilian sojourn. On the inside of his son's copy he wrote: "Sammy, I hope you take this trip someday. It changed my life. Love, Dad."

Sam later described his father as "a scientist, and indisputably proud of it, the 'father' of technology at Johnson Wax", an "internationalist" who created an "organization he could trust" so he could travel, enjoy himself and "still take care of the business details on an overseas journey". According to Sam, HF was "a creative leader" who "insisted on the best", drew superior performance from his people, and "believed in the benefits of retaining wise consultants and counsel", a man with a vision who thought in terms of entire generations, a "humanist" who believed in the good of individual creativity and in the "dignity of man and woman". Sam quotes his father as frequently saying: "Every community where we operate should become a better place because we are there." Sam remembered his father as "a family man who ... took his son hunting and fishing".

In 1953, HF wrote Sam a letter that was to be opened upon his death. Twenty-five years later Sam opened it:

Some people may try to challenge you by saying you are not doing as well as your grandfather or father did. This is something you should not give any worry to because what your great grandfather, grandfather and I did was to build on a foundation of honesty and integrity in business. Just go ahead in the way you think best. I'm confident in your future.

Sam (1928–) joined the business as his father's assistant in 1954, with a master's degree in business from Harvard Business School in his pocket and two years of US Air Force service. On the advice of a consulting firm (Booz, Allen and Hamilton), HF developed a career plan for Sam. Later, Sam recalled that he had been upset about having to follow a carefully laid-out development plan – after all, wasn't he the son of the owner and entitled to go straight to the top? But in time, he came to appreciate the wisdom of the incremental approach thought out by Jim Allen of Booz, Allen and Hamilton that initially had him directing a newly created department responsible for developing new products. The Johnson Wax Company had grown internationally, but it was still primarily limited to wax products for various applications. "I had just become the company's new products director, and our section had decided that the insecticide field was a good and growing business, one in which we wanted to play a part."

Sam recalls his first product idea:

> I had a mock label created, stuck it on a can, brought the sample of "Johnson's Aerosol Insecticide" to my father, and announced that this was a business we surely ought to enter. He looked at me and then at the can. "Don't you realize we don't make any products without wax in them?" he said. Although he was the boss, he was also my father, so I was able to risk a little impertinence and I answered, "Well, we could put a little wax in it, but I don't think it would do the product any good." My shot at humour didn't throw him off track. He told me we didn't know anything about bugs. I replied that we were learning. He said: "OK, then let's get down to fundamentals. Tell me what is better about that product than what is already on the market." I offered: "It will have a nice label and be an aerosol." He said, "Does it work *better* than the other ones?" I admitted finally: "No. It's just a darn good aerosol insecticide." My father replied, "Then take it back to the lab and when you have something that is better, come back and we'll talk about the insecticide business." His instincts were right and we did come back with a better insect killer: Raid. When we came out with an aqueous formula, we indeed had a Product Plus. It smelled better and killed insects without harming plants.

The following years saw a number of new products move the company away from the wax-related products: the Garden Bug Killer, Off (a mosquito repellent), Pledge (a furniture duster and polisher), and Glade air freshener. Within a year of market introduction, they represented 35 per cent of total domestic sales. The new product development process created by Sam was so innovative that it became the subject of a Harvard Business School case study, and stands today as a model for new product development organizations.

In 1959, Sam moved into international operations and travelled to Europe. In 1960, he was named European regional director, and in 1962, he was promoted to International vice president. Sam's first important setback occurred in 1965 when he oversaw the consolidation of European regional manufacturing in a large new plant in the Netherlands, an effort that was designed to reduce cost and improve efficiency. Faced with overcapacity, start-up problems and major losses, Sam was called back to the US. His father was furious about the bad results. Several weeks later, at the age of 65, Sam's father suffered a stroke that left him severely handicapped. He could neither read nor write well and became very irritable. Sam recalls, "I always wondered whether I had given him the stroke because of the mess-up I'd made in Europe."

In 1966, at 38, Sam became president of the company, which now boasted annual sales of US$171 million. His father, now honorary chairman, wintered in Florida, so Sam had to fly down every two weeks to report. These visits often turned very unpleasant. His increasingly irritable father often railed, "I don't like these numbers. And I don't like you either. And you're fired." Later, Sam recalled that this was a most difficult and depressing time. When his father died in 1978, Sam received the letter his father had written in 1953 for posthumous delivery. The 25-year-old letter "released [him] to be [himself] and not just a clone of [his] father".

By then, Sam had put his imprint as a strong leader on a company with revenues reaching US$1 billion in 1978. This was based on a strong, international expansion through diversification and acquisitions. He had decided on this approach during a one-year sabbatical he took in 1968 after his father's stroke. He also planned for the ownership transition from himself to his four children by setting up trusts for them and the grandchildren.

In 1976, in a statement of corporate philosophy entitled "This We Believe", Sam codified the basic principles that he believed drove the family business. It built on his grandfather's famous 1927 Christmas Profit Sharing speech:

Employees: We believe that the fundamental vitality and strength of our worldwide company lies in our people.

Consumers and users: We believe in earning the enduring goodwill of consumers and users of our products and services.

General public: We believe in being a responsible leader within the free market economy.

Neighbors and hosts: We believe in contributing to the well being of the countries and communities where we conduct business.

World community: We believe in improving international understanding.

Further to these principles, Sam added: "The way of safeguarding these beliefs is to remain a privately held company. Our way of reinforcing them is to make profits through growth and development, profits which allow us to do more for all the people on whom we depend." Dick Hansen, current CEO of Johnson Financial Group, talks about how these beliefs make a difference for employees in a family owned business: "I see Sam's integrity through his respect for the community. Sam challenges us to make our communities better because we are there. He doesn't talk values, he lives them."

One strong example for this values-based management approach occurred in 1975, when Sam Johnson voluntarily and unilaterally banned the worldwide use of chlorofluorocarbons (CFCs) from all Johnson aerosol products. At the time, unproven research suggested that CFCs might harm the ozone layer. Both internally and externally, Sam's decision was widely criticized until, three years later, it was validated when the US and Canada officially banned the use of CFCs in aerosols. It also turned out to be a smart business decision as company scientists discovered that propane was a cheaper substitute for CFCs, a strong advantage over competitors.

The business continued to grow in the consumer products field. In 1970, Johnson Diversified, now known as Johnson Outdoors Inc., was created, making leisure products like boats and camping equipment. The Johnson Bank was started in Wisconsin. These steps were made both out of fear and logic: fear of being cornered by larger, publicly held consumer products companies, like Procter & Gamble; logic by providing entrepreneurial opportunities in new businesses to the next generation of family business leaders.

Sam had married Imogene Powers, whom he had met in college, in 1954. Together they have four children: Curt (b. 1955), Helen (b. 1956), Fisk (b. 1958) and Winnie (b. 1959). All four were educated at Cornell, where the business school is called the Johnson School. Each of the children decided to join the family business without pressure from their father. Although they recognized the expectations and pressures put on next-generation members of the owning family, they felt the company was a special place. Like their father a generation before, they believed family leadership was necessary to ensure the core values – which led to its success – continued to guide the operations.

In 1985, Helen was the first member of the fifth generation to join the company as an associate product manager. In 1986, Winnie joined as a public affairs manager. One year later, Fisk joined the company as a marketing associate. And in 1990, Curt joined the company when Windpoint Ventures, a venture capital fund he started, was folded into the family business.

Late in his career, Sam began to suffer from the same addiction to alcohol his mother had once had. With strong support from his wife and children, he decided to confront this dependence. After a one-month treatment in 1993 in the Mayo Clinic, of which he was the chairman, he returned home cured, and readying himself for retirement from day-to-day responsibilities. He started to think about his father's journey to Brazil and what it had meant in his life. Recalling the note his father had left in his book expressing the hope that Sam would make the same journey one day, Sam decided to follow in his father's footsteps.

The original aircraft had been sold and crashed in Asia and could not be salvaged. Sam decided to have an exact replicate built, a project that took over three years. On 22 October 1998, Sam and his two sons, Curt and Fisk, took off from Racine, Wisconsin, for a month-long trip to the Brazilian rain forest, following the route of Sam's father well over 60 years earlier. There the rest of the family joined them. The trip proved to be an invigorating experience – much as it had been for his father. But Sam also wanted it filmed as a legacy for his family and companies. The film, *Carnauba: A Son's Memoir*, turned out much more personal than intended. In it, Sam speaks very openly about his father, himself and the difficult periods in their lives. Even his children had not understood the extent of Sam's difficulties with his father. Fisk said, "My brother and sisters and I have been huge beneficiaries of the relationship that my father had with his father. I think my father said to himself, 'I'm never going to put my children through this'." His brother Curt stated in an internet posting to the company employees: "The trip has provided us with an opportunity to talk about some of the issues and opportunities facing the family businesses. I feel connected to the visioning process my grandfather experienced when he made this trip."

By this time, the family had created a council with regular meetings of all family members to deal with both family and business matters. Sam had a strong interest in the history of family businesses; he knew well their fragile structures, and he devoted much attention to preparing next-generation family members and creating a large degree of transparency. The council became the forum for succession planning. It became increasingly apparent that the children had different interests and leadership aspirations. Sam, who had seen many family businesses suffer from sibling rivalry, wanted to avoid siblings reporting to each other. Without conflicts, the family arrived at a suitable arrangement in 1999.

Fisk, who has a PhD in applied physics, became chairman of SC Johnson, the core consumer products business. Helen became chairman of Johnson Outdoors Inc., the recreational products business. Curt became chairman of JohnsonDiversey, now the second largest institutional and industrial products and services business in the world. And Winnie, who had expressed a lesser interest in the business, became president of the Johnson Family Foundation. Helen described the functional separation as follows: "We each found our spot. Curt was the wheeler-dealer entrepreneur, Fisk was the technician, and I was the one interested in marketing."

In a joint statement, the four children talk about the relationship between the two generations:

> Under Dad's leadership, within just a few brief decades, the Johnson business went from a small wax company (US$171 million in sales) to four major global enterprises (combined US$8 billion in sales) that include household goods, innovative commercial products and services, environmentally-responsible polymers, diverse financial services and some of the most recognized brands in the recreational industry. And he didn't just champion the business. He took seriously the challenge of making our world a better place to live. Whether funding the restoration of Martin Luther King Junior's birthplace, contributing time and money to the World Business Council for Sustainable Development, or helping protect a unique ecosystem in Brazil, Dad has dedicated himself personally and positioned the family businesses to shape our communities and protect our planet. But even more important to us, his children, is the support Dad provides right here at home. From the family dining room to the corporate boardroom, he has been a coach, protector and friend to each of us. He has guided us with wise counsel, but also encouraged us to follow our hearts.

The Bonnier Group

2003 "IMD-Lombard Odier Darier Hentsch Distinguished Family Business Award" Winner
By Professor Joachim Schwass

The early generations

The Bonnier Group is a leading Scandinavian diversified-media conglomerate of over 200 privately owned companies. The ownership is in the hands of 73 family members from the fifth to the eighth generations who are direct descendants of the founding family. The family appears strongly committed to building and expanding a business that grew from modest beginnings when Gerhard Bonnier, the founder, opened a library in Copenhagen in 1804.

Gerhard Bonnier (1778–1862) was born in Germany as Gutkind Hirschel, son of a banker in Dresden. When he was 22, Bonnier migrated to Denmark. There, making a fresh start, he grew his modest library into a book publishing business. He married a Danish girl in 1803. They had eleven children. Adolf, the first-born, opened bookstores first in Gothenburg, Sweden (1827), in Uppsala and then in Stockholm. Another brother, David Felix, took over in Gothenburg; he later started the daily newspaper *Göteborgsposten*. Meanwhile, the youngest son, Albert, took multiyear training in various publishing firms in Scandinavia and abroad. In 1837, he opened his own Stockholm publishing firm, called Albert Bonniers Förlag, which became the platform for today's media group. The publishing business expanded, most notably at mid-century, with a backward integration of composition and printing. In the second generation 100 per cent ownership was maintained. From his operating profits, Albert invested in a printing house. This led to an initial investment in *Dagens Nyheter*, a leading Swedish daily newspaper. The next generation bought more shares in *Dagens Nyheter*, and in the 1920s, the family became the dominant owners.

Albert and Betty had three children: two daughters and a middle son, Karl Otto (1856–1941). Following the pattern of selecting the first-born male descendant, the parents viewed Karl Otto as the natural leader of the family company. At the death of his father in 1900, Karl Otto became the sole owner (his sisters received no shares in the business). The first three generations thus upheld a strict ownership strategy: total ownership control by one descendant, either prepared for this role, or by separation from other family members. While Gerhard had had the idea that the family should get involved in distributing books, the second generation, represented by Albert, pursued publishing. This laid the foundation for the culture that drives the family today: a strong interest in culture, and trusting, respectful relationships with authors. In the third generation, Karl Otto took the company in two directions:

- The business model was broadened to prepare for diversification into daily papers and magazines. The initial investment in *Dagens Nyheter* became a controlling interest in what, by that time, had become the largest daily paper in Sweden after World War I.
- The family as a driver for the business and a guarantor of the values greatly increased with a move to a stately family home in an elegant part of Stockholm. The home, which was called Nedre Manilla ("lower Manilla"), quickly became a focal point in the lives of all future Bonnier generations. Karl Otto expanded the building for his ever-growing art collection. He and his wife, Lisen, raised their six children in Manilla and used it for social gatherings and business, often entertaining Bonnier Group authors. The Bonnier children attended many of these dinners and grew up with intellectual curiosity and cultural education, and gradually the boundaries between family life and business life faded.

In the fourth generation, Karl Otto's first son, Tor (1883–1976), assumed both business and family leadership. Daughters were again excluded from the family business. Once married, they left Manilla, and lost their informal contact with the business and Bonnier authors. At Karl Otto's death, the two daughters inherited some real estate, but business ownership went to Tor, Åke and Kaj (a fourth son, Gert, was pursuing an academic career). The distribution of ownership was slightly decreasing following birth order. After three generations of ownership concentrated in one hand, for the first time, a new rule came into play: male descendants who were working in the family business received ownership. This working partnership model, however, was in no way egalitarian – Tor dominated. Åke moved to the United States. Kaj assumed leadership of the Bonnier's traditional book publishing. The applied ownership principle represented a mix of primo genitur and "operative partners" rules.

The fourth generation rigorously pursued the new, enlarged business model: under Tor's leadership the magazine publishing firm Åhlen & Åkerlund was acquired in 1929. This was a milestone for the family business. Until then, it had, for the most part, grown organically, or through gradual investments in the newspaper business with inherited capital. Acquiring Åhlen & Åkerlund was a big risk: the price of well over €1.0 million equalled the approximate value of the family business. The acquisition soon became a benchmark: future Bonnier generations revisited it whenever they were considering large investments.

The Bonnier family business was now in book publishing, newspaper editing and weekly magazines editing. The public image of the family business was, nevertheless, still associated with book publishing; when, in the 1940s, this branch of the business had been producing significant losses for more than two decades, the family never questioned its long-term publishing commitment and subsidized its publishing interests with profits from the well-run newspaper and magazine divisions. But internally, the family was growing more critical of Kaj's leadership. In 1952, Kaj asked to be bought out by Tor and Åke, and his shares were distributed pro rata parte. Taking account of the initial unequal shareholding, this brought Tor to about 54 per cent ownership, and Åke, who was still living in the United States, now had 46 per cent. And so, at this time, the family business returned to a dominant owner stage, the model on which it had been founded.

The impact of a growing family on ownership

Tor had married three times. He had three boys with his first wife Greta: Albert Jr (Abbe), Johan and Lukas. The next two marriages produced three more male descendants: Simon, Karl-Adam and Mikael. Åke, Tor's brother, had one son only, Gerard, which simplified the ownership inheritance. But Tor's situation was more complicated. During his first divorce, his first wife, Greta, strongly defended the ownership rights of her sons. Each received a third each of Tor's shares, with Abbe, the eldest, getting an additional 1 per cent so his siblings would see him as the dominant leader. When the younger half-brothers were born, each of the eldest brothers gave 1 per cent of their shares to them. From two owners in the fourth generation, the family business now had seven owners in the fifth generation with very unequal shareholdings, both inter- and intrabranch. To gain clarity and commitment, a 50-year ownership contract was drawn up along the following lines:

- The family wanted to stay together and build the business
- Family members who wanted to sell were not allowed to go outside the family.

While other cousins pursued outside careers, in the fifth generation, management responsibilities were divided among Abbe, Lukas and Gerard as follows:

- Abbe looked after the newspaper business and emerged as the leader, with a strong entrepreneurial drive
- Lukas looked after the magazine business
- Gerard became head of book publishing.

Lukas said of this arrangement between the cousins: "In a way, we did not need a paper contract. The bond was strong. We wanted to stay together and had more than enough trust in each other."

Building on his father's diversification strategy, Abbe added a daily evening paper to *Dagens Nyheter*, which continued to be very successful. In 1944, *Expressen* was launched. By now, the Bonnier family business had such a strong position in publishing and editing in Sweden that public concern was growing: the family, it was said, was too powerful. Abbe was troubled by the danger this perception might entail. Being growth oriented, he adopted the view that the family's future was in unrelated diversification, away from Swedish media. So, starting in the early 1950s, Abbe launched a more than three-decade expansion. The Group made initial investments in vertically related industries like paper. Increasingly though, the Bonnier family invested in and acquired companies in unrelated industries like furniture production, disposable tableware, packaging, engineering and ferry services. When younger members of the family talk about Abbe's enormous entrepreneurial drive, they tell of the time Abbe travelled to the southern tip of Latin America where he discovered shrimp farming and immediately wanted to enter that business. Lukas said: "Abbe was unstoppable. But he did consult with his cousin Gerard, the single largest owner, before making any investment. And there was good corporate back-up by a solid finance director."

While fourth-generation Tor was approaching his seventies and reducing his workload, in the early 1950s, Abbe shifted the responsibility of the traditional businesses to Lukas and Gerard. They enjoyed freedom to run the newspaper, magazine and book publishing businesses as they saw fit. Abbe got involved only when the two of them faced difficulties or needed money. By 1957, Abbe saw his main responsibility as managing the concern and diversification projects. But his entrepreneurial energy and enthusiasm spilled over to the non-family managers he had put at the top of newly acquired companies.

CEO selection and appointment was the most important vehicle for the owning family to influence the growing business. Although the family's ownership interests were combined in a holding company over which Abbe presided, there was no formal governance structure. Abbe was the leader; he made all key decisions. He was constantly travelling and visiting the various companies, often with his wife, Birgit, who played an important role in many of his business decisions. She provided input and advice and often evaluated potential candidates for management positions after private dinners with them and their wives.

Abbe's summerhouse in Dalarö, on the coast south of Stockholm, was the venue for many dinner parties with business associates, employees and family members. In good family tradition, the children participated in these parties and celebrations, meeting business people and following the elders' business discussions. Decision making was, therefore, highly centralized, but always carefully checked with the other family shareholders, particularly Gerard, who was now the largest owner. Gerard had carved himself a strong leadership position in the publishing business from which he aptly represented the family's interests. He kept up steady contact with leading writers and artists and maintained and grew the family's art collection.

By the mid-1970s, with new legislation requiring employee representation on corporate boards, the Bonnier family's decision process needed to change. Soon, decisions were taken more formally, but the family came to board meetings with one voice and a consensus reached in previous informal consultations, often during family meals.

Abbe continued the industrial diversification, financing it entirely from cash the family's businesses generated. This meant that the traditional publishing business had a hard time, since it could have benefited from the financial resources that were flowing to the industrial companies. In 1976, a new financial paper was launched: *Dagens Industri*. Initially it was seen as a weekly technical information sheet, but in 1980, after accumulated losses, the Group positioned it as a business paper published three days a week, then five, and finally six. Hasse Olsson, who today heads the Bonnier Business Press division, recalls:

> When I joined the Dagens Industri paper in 1980 there were 35 people. Today there are 9 business papers in different European countries employing 1200 people. Until the advertising slump in 2000, we were consistently the most profitable business paper with gross profit margins of 40 percent.

In 1978, Abbe stepped up from working president to working chairman of the Group. He was 71, but still very much in control. Since no family member was ready for the presidency, a non-family outsider was chosen. Until Abbe's death in 1989, there were two non-family presidents, no doubt because it was difficult to work under an active, powerful chairman. This governance structure, born of necessity, later became the new model for the family: either a family member or a non-family member would hold the chairmanship and the presidency respectively; thus, power between ownership and management was balanced. Abbe held the chairmanship until 1988, at which time his younger brother Lucas succeeded him (he remained for four years).

The sixth generation arrives

The sixth generation was growing up, and there were more family members now. The Tor and Åke branches, which had grown to seven male descendants and owners in the fifth generation, had now evolved to 28 male and female descendants in the sixth generation. For the first time, female descendants were entitled not only to ownership but also to employment in the business. In fact, Abbe, Lucas and Gerard agreed that it was good to have many next-generation family members work in the business in order to see who emerged as the key candidate for leadership in the sixth generation. Abbe did not seem to be overly concerned with succession planning. He also had two daughters, which according to family tradition meant that a male nephew would succeed him. And so it was Carl-Johan, the third son of Abbe's brother Johan, who became the next-generation leader. Born in 1951, Carl-Johan entered the family business right after taking a business degree at Stockholm School of Economics. He said:

> There were no real succession discussions in the family. It just happened that several of the sixth generation members entered the business in various functions. For me, it was just natural and easy to enter the family business because it seemed so much more interesting than any other business.

Succession from the fifth to the sixth generation represented an enormous paradigm shift ("breakpoint") for the family and for the business. Up through the fifth generation, the concept of the dominant owner had prevailed. Ownership and management control was limited – by choice – to as few persons as possible. Even though the number of owners had grown, the consensus was that there had to be one dominant leader. Reflecting on reasons why the family business had survived for so many generations, the sixth-generation family members agreed on the following explanations:

- Ownership was never an issue. Each inheritor understood that he would hold ownership for the next generation.
- A strong consensus approach combined with a "communication culture". Family members raised business issues in their informal meetings, and when a member seriously objected to a project, it was dropped.
- Interest in the business was nurtured in most family members from a young age.

Lukas reflected on this breakpoint for the family business:

> When I was chairman, after the strong and entrepreneurial leadership of Abbe, I believed that the only way forward for our enormously diversified business and

for the very large number of sixth generation family members would be to go public. I sincerely believed that we had reached the limits as a family business. But I had not counted on the energy and enthusiasm of the next generation. They persuaded me that they were ready, willing and able to take our privately held family business to a new level, by building on the tradition, but in an innovative, different way. I changed my mind and encouraged them to do it.

Managing a complicated generational transition

In the early 1990s, the sixth generation members – together with Lukas – went through an educational programme about family business structures and strategies, which created a platform for learning, discussion and development. The programme provided a common language for the large sixth-generation family group and allowed them to create a vision of how the family would keep adding value. Carl-Johan emerged as the natural leader and was appointed CEO in 1991. Lukas Bonnier soon thereafter stepped down as chairman of the board and was replaced by a trusted non-family former executive.

The business model Abbe had created now came under pressure. The diversification strategy had stretched financial resources and human resources to the limits. The once tightly controlled media market in Sweden had opened up, and the internet offered enormous opportunities. The sixth generation rapidly concluded that it should focus on the traditional industry – media – and capitalize on new opportunities there, instead of spreading resources thinly across the unrelated diversified industries. In Carl-Johan's words, "The family had a name in media – the family always liked the publishing of books, papers and magazines; therefore, it was an easy decision to pull out of the wide diversification and instead focus nationally and internationally on the business that is in the blood of the family." Until 1998, there were a number of divestitures, and the proceeds went to expanding the media businesses and acquiring related companies.

Another turning point came in 1998 when the family considered increasing its investment in Marieberg, a publicly traded publishing business in which it held just under 50 per cent ownership. The Bonnier Group already had substantial business dealings with Marieberg, and merging the activities made strategic sense. Marieberg's revenues were similar to the Bonnier Group's, so the investment would be a very sizeable financial commitment. The Bonnier family essentially had two choices:

- Merge the Bonnier Group into the publicly traded Marieberg company, thus providing access to further growth capital on a public stock market and providing family members with exit opportunities, or
- Take Marieberg private and merge it into the Bonnier Group (still 100 per cent privately owned by the Bonnier family).

The Bonnier cousins preferred the second option. They feared that going to the stock market could increase the risk of the family business breaking up over time. The emotional attachment to the media industry, and more specifically to the traditional book publishing business, was so strong that the family was willing to pay the price of this acquisition. In fact, the overall purchasing package was close to €500 million, which represented about half of the Bonnier Group's assets. In order to finance the project, bank loans were negotiated and several assets were sold. Within 12 months, half of the borrowings were repaid. This project reflects the continuing entrepreneurial drive in the owning family. Several times in earlier generations the family had proven to be willing to accept large risks by acquiring large companies, which helped them, each time, take the family business to a new platform.

The Bonnier Group: modern business structures

Through this acquisition, the head of Marieberg, Bengt Braun, joined the Bonnier Group. He became group president and CEO, and Carl-Johan Bonnier became executive chairman of the board. Braun had had a successful career with Procter & Gamble before taking over at Marieberg in 1989. He brought experience of a structured organization and management competence to the Bonnier Group, the media activities of which are now divided into six distinct business divisions:

- Books
- Magazine Group
- Business Press
- Newspapers
- Business Information
- Entertainment

A president who reports directly to Bengt Braun heads each division. In order to maximize freedom and initiative in the six divisions, the size and functions of the Group head office have been drastically reduced. The head office functions include Group Finance and Group Human Resources. At the top of the hierarchy, Carl-Johan Bonnier, representing the family owners, and Bengt Braun, the non-family CEO, share the power. To facilitate frequent, close contact, Bonnier and Braun have adjoining offices on the same floor of the Bonnier building in Stockholm.

The important generational transition in the 1990s brought two family issues to the fore:

- The family was rapidly growing – 28 descendants in the sixth generation, and the seventh generation likely to be a multiple of this. The family would be more and more widely dispersed around the globe, with only a fraction of the younger family members living in the Stockholm area.
- The old shareholder agreement from 1952, binding family owners together, would expire in the year 2000.

The sixth-generation family members realized that the three-year transition from the fifth to the sixth generation had produced an effective outcome for the family and the business because they had jointly built a transparent decision-making process that involved all family members. Contrary to the prevailing centralized decision making by one leader in all previous generations, the family now required an institutional – but effective – approach to exercising responsible ownership and management power over a growing business empire.

A new approach to governance

The family constructed a new approach to governance that rests on two pillars:

- *On the business side*: Albert Bonnier AB combines the family ownership interests in a holding company, which has 12 family members (seven ordinary and five deputy members) plus three honorary family members on the board. The operating company, Bonnier AB, fully owned by the holding company, has a board with five family members who are nominated by the holding company board, five non-family members and three employee representatives, as required by law. This board decides on any investment larger than €2 million. Today, the chairman of both the holding and operating companies is Carl-Johan Bonnier.
- *On the family side*: the Bonnier Family Foundation takes care of all family issues. The foundation has a board of eight family members, six from the general assembly and two from the holding company board, plus the company chairman. The chairman of the family foundation is sixth-generation Hans-Jacob Bonnier, who holds a six-year mandate.

In the hierarchy, a general assembly is above the business holding company and the family foundation. The general assembly today includes all 73 family owners who meet once a year for a full day meeting preceded by a dinner the night before. This "owners day" is attended by the owners (with or without spouses), non-family board members and the company management officers. The general assembly elects the holding company board and chairman, and the family foundation board. Family members exercise their voting rights in two ways:

- *On the ownership side*: their votes are weighed according to the percentage of shares each family member owns
- *On the family foundation side*: each family member has one vote.

The Bonnier Family Foundation has become a meaningful, well-structured institution whose mission is to keep the family together and actively involved in a range of activities that go beyond ownership. The board, which meets five times a year, is elected every two years in order to allow a broad involvement of many family members. A number of activities and committees exist:

- *Family mansion committee*: looks after the family home Manilla with its portrait gallery, renovations and rules for the utilization by family members
- *Financial Committee*: sets up budgets for the family foundation
- *Education committee*: formalizes and transmits the family's owner philosophy, to arrange trainee and summer jobs and scholarships
- *Family social events*: golf tournaments, Christmas party, cinema previews, and so on
- *Family archives*: keep track of the large number of family documents and publications
- *Gutkind & Company*: a next-generation activity.

Gutkind & Company came into being in the late 1990s as a formal initiative to prepare and educate the young next-generation family members for ownership. The agenda is based on education and fun. In 2003, there are 28 members who are 16–32 years old. They have their own board with seven members elected every year, which allows regular rotation and training of board functions and formalities. The chairman is automatically a deputy in the Bonnier Family Foundation. The activities include two yearly educational seminars, one of which lasts three days. The members have their own Website for easy contact in between meetings. The family foundation chairman, Hans-Jacob Bonnier, who initiated this activity, recalls how the first meeting was launched:

> We wanted to create a strong bonding between these young family members who did not all know each other. So we put them on a boat going to a barbecue on one of the islands outside Stockholm. We staged a technical engine problem so all had to organize themselves in an emergency situation. That really got them going, and the whole event became more dynamic and fun!

The family ownership philosophy

On the general assembly level, in 1998, the family unanimously signed a new shareholder agreement, well before the 50-year agreement expired in 2001. The new agreement is valid for 30 years (until 2030). The underlying philosophy of this agreement introduced new elements:

- The family does not want to think in terms of branches, which might endanger unity
- The contractual period of 30 years is sufficiently long for the current sixth and seventh generations to protect their unity, but short enough so that the following generation can freely decide on their own ownership structure
- An internal market for shares, first between family members and only secondly with the family foundation, based on a clear formula.

The family also defined their ownership philosophy:

- "We want to be responsible owners with high integrity, moral and ethical standards"
- The family is guided by the traditional family values: "Servants of free speech, responsibility and quality"
- The family wants to stay together and be loyal to the majority
- A moderate dividend policy
- Hire the best professionals to run the business
- Provide job opportunities for family members.

Hans-Jacob Bonnier comments on the ownership philosophy: "For me, my grandfather's statement that we are in the business *to be servants of free speech* has really meant a lot."

In 2003, 12 family members were working on different levels in the Group. No one family member reports to another family member. Marcus Forsell, a seventh-generation family member who heads the activities in radio, said that, "As family members we have to prove more and work harder than non-family employees."

The non-family president, Bengt Braun, notes that,

> It is in the company's interest – and mine as a president – to have more family members work in the business. The family knows that they must be competent

for the job, of course. And, as family members, they bring a deep-seated commitment and understanding which is good for all.

Conclusion

In 2003, just one year before the Bonnier Group celebrates its 200th anniversary, the sixth and seventh generations appear to be firmly committed to the future as a family business. The Group has governance structures in place – both for the business and for the family – that they use actively and to ensure transparency, commitment and emotional attachment to the business. This represents a logical evolution since the first generation. Chairman Carl-Johan Bonnier states:

> Clearly, we have survived so many generations because the business has always been successful. In addition, our industry is exciting, glamorous and fun, and makes it attractive for family members to work. Of course they must be competent and follow the rules. I am convinced the business will continue to perform for another generation. If it is still a family owned business – that is up to each coming generation to decide.

This article was written by Professor Joachim Schwass, IMD, based on interviews with fifth, sixth and seventh generation family members and senior non-family management of the Bonnier Group.

The Barilla Group

2004 IMD-Lombard Odier Darier Hentsch Distinguished Family Business Award
By Professor Joachim Schwass

Barilla is a household name all over the globe, and the family behind the name has recently been awarded the 2004 IMD-Lombard Odier Darier Hentsch Distinguished Family Business Award. The Barilla Group is not only the largest Italian food processing business but also the world market leader for pasta products. The business is controlled by the fourth generation of direct descendants of the founder Pietro Barilla.

The beginnings

In 1877, Pietro Barilla, then in his twenties, opened a bakery shop in the centre of Parma, Italy, where he sold bread and pasta. He produced the pasta in a traditional way using a small wooden press; the maximum daily capacity was 50 kilogrammes. With the support of his wife, and by working 18-hour days, Pietro grew the business slowly but steadily. Expansion into a second shop did not succeed, so he focused on developing the pasta production. He specialized in egg pasta, which differentiated his business from the mainstream offerings that used just flour and water. By 1900, he was using five wooden presses and five ovens. Ten years later, the first factory was built, employing 80 workers. This factory was run by Pietro's two sons, Riccardo and Gualtiero, the second generation, who were then in their thirties.

The second generation

Riccardo and Gualtiero had worked alongside their father since they were 14 years old. In 1914, the two brothers took the unusual step of launching a marketing campaign with posters showing Barilla pasta with a mother and child. The objective was to reach the consumer directly and create demand for Barilla products.

While Riccardo was in charge of production, Gualtiero looked after sales. He emerged as the entrepreneur and risk taker. He wanted to be a missionary and never married, but his father pushed him to join the business, where he had a reputation for taking good care of the employees. But in 1919, Gualtiero died suddenly and unexpectedly from food poisoning. Ownership reverted to Riccardo, thus returning the family business in the second generation to the owner-manager structure that had prevailed with the founder, with 100 per cent control in the hands of one family member.

The business continued to grow. In Parma, Barilla pasta was sold through company stores; in the rest of Italy, it was sold through grocers with exclusivity contracts. Following participation in international trade fairs, there were a few minor exports. World War I had led to a shortage of meat, and pasta was increasingly seen as an inexpensive but nutritious alternative.

The third generation

Riccardo, with the help of his wife, Virginia, and his two sons, Pietro and Gianni, continued to invest in both updating the production equipment and building the brand. By 1936, 700 workers were producing 80 tons of pasta and 15 tons of bread per day using six continuous presses. As in the previous generation, the functional responsibilities were split into technical (Gianni) and commercial (Pietro). The problems started when Pietro, the more entrepreneurially oriented of the two brothers, was drafted into military service in 1939 when World War II broke out. During this time, the government directed food production primarily to the army, and the consumer-based distribution system that Barilla had ably built up over decades was starved of supplies. Air raids also damaged part of the plant. Meanwhile, Pietro Barilla was driving trucks for the Italian army at the Russian Front. His son Paolo later said that the time during the war had greatly shaped his father's character: "He saw poverty, death and human misery. That certainly put everything else in perspective."

When he returned from the war, Pietro and his brother Gianni started to rebuild the business. For them, 1947 was an important year. Sadly, their father Riccardo died. They cancelled the supply contract with the Italian army and developed a new distribution system throughout the Italian peninsula by acquiring a fleet of small trucks. In 1950, Pietro visited the United States to study American marketing practices. As a result, they stopped bread production in 1952 in order to focus exclusively on pasta. The Italian graphic artist Erberto Carboni created a new trademark for Barilla, inspired by the white and yolk of an egg lying on its side. This was adopted as the firm's logo and is, after several evolutionary changes, still in use today. In 1955, Barilla was the first manufacturer to pack pasta in portion-sized cardboard boxes. The consumer market was growing again. In 1960, Barilla became a joint-stock company. By this time, there were 1,300 workers and a sales team of 200. In 1965, Barilla opened a new plant for non-perishable baked goods, such as breadsticks and rusks. Four years later, the company built the world's largest pasta manufacturing plant in Pedrignano, with a surface area of 1.25 million square metres. The production capacity was 1,000 tons a day.

The breakpoint

The completion of the plant coincided with one of Italy's darkest periods. Having overheated in the 1950s, the economy now paid the price through enormous inflation. Political and social unrest grew. A spate of terrorism with almost daily victims and kidnappings created uncertainty and unrest. Many companies went bankrupt or were sold. Gianni Barilla felt that they should sell the business and leave the country, but Pietro wanted none of that. Gianni, who held 50 percent of the business, offered his share to Pietro, who said he could not buy his brother out. In 1971, the 94-year-old family business was sold to the US multinational, Grace, which wanted to enter the food market in Italy. While Gianni moved to Switzerland, Pietro – who had reluctantly agreed to accept the offer from Grace – stayed in Parma. His sons later commented about this period: "The sale broke our father's heart. He loved the business. And he had only one thing in mind – how to regain control of the business."

Grace undertook several strategic moves with the Barilla Company, which were important for the future:

- 1972: entered the milling sector with the acquisition of a first mill in Italy
- 1973: purchased the Voiello pasta factory, taking Barilla's market share in Italy to 15 per cent
- 1975: created the Mulino Bianco line of baked products that taught Italians a whole new way of thinking about breakfast
- 1977: extended the Mulino Bianco line to include fresh products: snacks, mini-cakes and soft sliced bread.

By 1979, the company had sales of €130 million and employed 1,600 people. But Grace was not satisfied with its entry into the Italian food market and put the company up for sale. Pietro Barilla, who had never given up hope of regaining ownership, worked feverishly to raise the necessary capital. For many months he commuted between Italy and New York. Once, his son Guido recalled, he felt so close to achieving his dream of recapturing the family's business but did not make it and broke down in tears. Finally, Pietro succeeded in buying back the company from the US multinational. His children recalled this period:

> We were very young then, in our teens. But we understood how much our father was emotionally attached to the business and that he must have suffered when it was sold to Grace. But at home, he was always a warm, caring and positive father.

Pietro was 66 years old in 1979, but appeared to have boundless energy. Both he and the workers were enthusiastic, and a strong period of growth started. This time, the economic environment was considerably better than it had been a decade earlier. The government lifted the ceiling on the price of pasta, which had been one of the key irritation factors for Grace. Once again, the pasta market became attractive for manufacturers. In 1985, Barilla launched a creative marketing campaign with the Italian filmmaker Federico Fellini, which involved many Italian and international stars over the years. In 1989, a new line of pasta sauces was launched. Two years later, Barilla made a strategic move outside of Italy by purchasing Misko, the leading pasta manufacturer in Greece. The following year, Barilla bought Pavesi, the famous and historic bakery company in Novara, Italy. And then, in 1993, at the age of 80, Pietro Barilla died, leaving the company of 8,500 employees and 25 factories to his four children. Barilla Group revenues amounted to about €2 billion. After three generations of dominant owners, the siblings shared equal ownership of the 85 per cent their father had held. A new era began.

The fourth generation

The fourth generation consisted of Guido (1958), Luca (1960), Paolo (1961) and Emanuela (1968). The two eldest children joined Barilla in their early twenties, shortly after their father had bought back the company. They both moved through various training phases in Italy and abroad and joined the board in 1987 as vice chairmen. Guido studied economy and philosophy and lived in New York for over two years. There he developed a strong interest in the US market and marketing practices. He joined the company's Barilla France subsidiary in 1982. Luca completed his education and management training in the US. In 1984, he joined the management team as a product manager, and the following year he gained direct sales experiences with Barilla France in Paris. In 1987, he became a member of the board of directors, assuming the role of executive vice chairman in 1988, together with Guido. He has been managing director of GranMilan since 1998.

Paolo was fascinated by professional motor racing and became a successful driver, winning the Le Mans 24-hour race in 1985 in the prototype category. He spent two years in Japan working for Toyota. There he gained strong insights into the principles of industrial quality. His father had agreed to support Paolo's ambition on two conditions: firstly, that his siblings were supportive of Paolo and, secondly, that he took this move seriously and professionally and gave it his best. When Paolo turned 30 he decided to return to Barilla, joining the French affiliate before moving to Italy. He joined the board in 1993. Emanuela pursued a career as a journalist but maintained a close interest in the business.

Guido and Paolo mentioned several key principles that their father had taught them all:

- The business can only be truly successful if it improves the life of people
- The richness of man is the work – not the money, which is only a tool to go through life
- Have clarity on what you do and make it readable to the outside.

When their father died, the siblings made it clear that they would jointly continue to develop the family business according to the entrepreneurial spirit of the previous three generations. But they also wanted to introduce new ways of managing the growing business. Their father had run the business in a very paternalistic way. His soul can still be felt in the business headquarters in Parma, where photos show him in the plant and where his impressive art collection adorns the gardens, offices, hallways and boardroom. To support the professionalization process, the brothers brought in a senior, highly experienced outsider. In 1995, former Procter & Gamble CEO Edwin Artzt joined Barilla as CEO for three years. He brought structures, clarity, cost management and marketing expertise. In 1996, the siblings decided to aggressively enter the US market and built a state-of-the-art pasta factory, costing more than €100 million, in Iowa. They decided to import Italian pasta taste standards rather than adapt to existing US pasta tastes. Just three years after market entry, Barilla was market leader for pasta in the US. Thanks to its high quality and a very effective marketing campaign, Barilla continued to grow in this important market. Marketing took up 4 per cent of the revenue. Other benchmarks during the first decade under the fourth generation included:

- 1994: acquisition of the number two pasta factory in Turkey
- 1997: construction of a new pasta factory in Italy, and launch of ready-to-use sauce products

- 1998: construction of a new pasta factory in Greece
- 1999: acquisition of Wasa, Europe's leading manufacturer of crispbreads.

Many other innovations, acquisitions and upgradings took place. A particularly remarkable move was the acquisition of the German Kamps Group in 2002. The Barilla siblings showed their commitment to entrepreneurial growth and a willingness to take certain risks – like previous generations before them – by staging a hostile €1.8 billion takeover of this publicly traded group of bread manufacturing and distribution companies in Germany and France. The Kamps Group had been built up by an entrepreneur who had bought many smaller companies, and it was experiencing structural and financial problems. Barilla, which had attained worldwide leadership in the pasta industry, saw this as an opportunity to strengthen geographic distribution weaknesses in the important German and French markets, and to substantially broaden its presence in the bread market. In many ways, this represented a return to the roots of the company, which had started 125 years earlier in both pasta and bread. The acquisition was financed with the support of several financial institutions, which held 49 per cent in Kamps, against the Barilla majority of 51 per cent. The brothers openly state that more work needs to be done in order to bring Kamps up to where it should be in terms of performance. Meanwhile, growth activities continue in other parts of the group. In 2004, the group employed 25,000 people, with group revenues of €4.4 billion and EBITDA (earnings before interest tax depreciation amortization) of €503 million (11.4 per cent of sales). The organizational structure shows a 100 per cent family-owned holding with four subsidiaries:

- Barilla G + R Fratelli S.p.A (84.75 per cent)
- GranMilan S.p.A (100 per cent)
- Harry's (100 per cent)
- Kamps (51 per cent).

The family-controlled holding has a board with all four siblings as directors – with Guido as chairman – and four non-family directors. The siblings are also active on the boards of each subsidiary with a number of independent directors. Each subsidiary has its own CEO and management team.

Table A.2 Barilla Group revenues and EBITDA per subsidiary in 2003

	Revenues (€ million)	EBITDA (€ million)
Barilla	2507	322
Kamps	1495	131
Harry's	239	29
GranMilan	194	25

Adding value in the fourth generation

The brothers' governance philosophy is "Influence but don't interfere". In addition to their ownership role on the different boards, they are present in three key committees:

- *The brand equity committee*: here, together with management, they discuss and jointly define the direction with regard to the brand ("everything you see")
- *The product development committee*: this committee decides on the launch of new products and the upgrade of existing ones
- *The category review committee*: this committee regularly reviews the business and financial performance of each business and product category.

The non-family CEO of Barilla, Gianluca Bolla, says that it is good for the business to have knowledgeable and visible owners. In fact, in 2003, the family published a booklet entitled "Changing to last", which formally states the views and the vision of the owning family. They expressed their intention to grow the business by "considering its original, founding values, meaning curiosity and passion stimulating the mind and expressing a concept capable of combining imagination and pragmatic thinking". According to Guido Barilla, the organization needs to be pushed and driven by new products, otherwise it runs the risk of becoming too self-centred. The family is both the driving force of this innovation and the guarantor of traditional values, including the safety of their products. They have stated their opposition to genetically modified organisms (GMOs). "There are too many questions and not enough answers. We cannot guarantee our food products to the consumer when we do not understand all risks."

The four siblings in the fourth generation seem at ease with the future. They draw on each other to build individual strength. They still live together in the group of houses their father built for the family in Parma, which facilitates frequent informal contact. They have made it clear that they will never sell the company or go public. In the words of Guido Barilla: "We are not a family business one can write a novel about, we are committed to simple, basic values and a daily discipline and process of constant improvement."

Professor Joachim Schwass, IMD, wrote this article based on publications of the Barilla Group; Les Echos 27 August 2001; "Barilla", by Monica Wagen in F.B.N. Newsletter, No. 23, May 1999, and interviews with the family and Gianluca Bolla.

References

Grant, Jeremy and Roberts, Adrienne (2001) "Swiss grain trader counts the cost of family ties: The restructuring of Andre has failed", *Financial Times*, 4 April.

Grow, Gerald (1988) "New Perspectives on Andragogy" in Malcolm S. Knowles, Elwood F. Holton III and Richard A. Swanson, *The Adult Learner* (5th edn.). Houston: Gulf Publishing Company.

Hill, Lillian H. (2001) "The Brain and Consciousness: Sources of Information for Understanding Adult Learning" in Sharan B. Merriam (ed.) *The New Update on Adult Learning Theory*. San Francisco: Jossey-Bass.

IMD-Lombard Odier Family Business Center (2001) *Keeping the Business in the Family: A Study of Swiss Family Businesses*. Lausanne, Switzerland.

Kellerman, Barbara (2004) *Bad Leadership*. Boston: Harvard Business School Press.

Kolb, D.A. (1984) *Experiential Learning: Experience on the Source of Learning and Development*. Englewood Cliffs: Prentice Hall.

Schwass, Joachim (2005) "Understanding the Successor's Challenges and an Effective Successor Development Strategy", in John L. Ward (ed.) *Unconventional Wisdom – Counterintuitive Insights for Family Business Success* Chichester: John Wiley.

Useem, Jerry (2004) "Another Boss – Another Revolution", *Fortune*, 5 April.

Vermot, P. (2001) "André & Cie Pousse Son Chant de Cygne et Met Fin à ses Activités Commerciales", *Agefi*, 12 March.

Index

Compiled by Sue Carlton

AD Little 16, 117
Åhlen & Åkerlund 20, 128
Albert Bonniers Förlag 19, 127
Ambadi Estates 115–16
AMM Foundation 16, 116
Andersen, Vagn Holck 86
André, Georges 30–1
André Group 30–1
André, Henri 31
Artzt, Edwin 140
award winning family businesses
    best practices 7, 8–9, 10–11, 13, 15, 17, 19, 21, 22
    lessons from 2–4
    success factors 1–2, 48

Barilla family
    Emanuela 139, 140
    Gianni 21–2, 138–9
    Gualtiero 21, 137
    Guido 57, 139–40, 142
    Luca 139–40
    Paolo 57, 138, 139, 140
    Pietro (founder) 21, 137
    Pietro (son of Riccardo) 21–2, 50, 70, 138–9
    Riccardo 21, 137, 138
    Virginia 21, 138
Barilla France 140
Barilla Group 21–2, 137–42
    acquisitions 22, 139, 140–1
    financial difficulties 22, 138–9
    governance structure 22, 140–2
    leadership transition 70
    and non-family CEO 22, 140, 142
    philanthropic activities 55
    sold to Grace 22, 139
Billund Airport 55, 86
Bloomingdale's 57, 109
Bolla, Gianluca 142
Bonnier AB 134

Bonnier family
    Abbe 20, 129–31
    Åke 20, 128–9
    Albert 19, 127–8
    Birgit 130
    Carl-Johan 20, 131, 132, 133, 134, 136
    David Felix 127
    Gerard 129, 130
    Gerhard (founder) 19, 127
    Hans-Jacob 134, 135
    Kaj 20, 128
    Karl Otto 19–20, 127–8
    Lukas 129, 130, 131–2
    Tor 20, 128–9, 130
Bonnier Family Foundation 134, 135
Bonnier Group 19–21, 127–36
    acquisitions 20, 76, 129, 132–3
    diversification 74, 129–30, 132
    female descendants 127, 128, 131
    governance structures 20, 56, 130, 133–5
    leadership transition 131–3
    and non-family managers 130, 131, 133, 134
    ownership 20, 27, 129, 130–1, 135–6
    philanthropic activities 55
Booz, Allen and Hamilton 18, 62
Braun, Bengt 133, 135–6
BSA 115
Burmese national movements 15, 114
business growth strategies 2, 72–7
    diversification 72, 73, 74
    evolutionary growth 24, 49
    internationalization 72, 73, 74
    vertical integration 72, 73, 74–5
    see also 'wise growth' strategy

Cano, Javier 10, 95, 98
Carboni, Erberto 138

Carborundum Universal of Madras, India (CUMI) 114, 115–16, 117
Carborundum USA 114
Carnauba: A Son's Memoir 125
carnauba palm tree 122
Chevron 115
chlorofluorocarbons (CFCs) 125
Cholamandalam 117
Chopard 82
Christiansen, Godtfred Kirk 6, 85, 86
Christiansen, Ole Kirk 5, 84
CIFCO 115–16, 120
Compass Management (CM) 87
CoRomendel Fertilizers Ltd 115–16
Corporacion Puig 9–11, 93–8
   acquisition 9, 10, 93
   advisory board 97
   diversification 93, 94
   dividend policy 95
   family protocol 96–7
   governance structure 10, 95–6, 98
   internationalization 9–10, 94
   and leadership development 62, 66
   leadership transition 61, 67–8, 69, 98
   and non-family CEO 10, 95, 98
   product development 94
   values 96
   see also Puig family
corporate citizenship/philanthropy 6, 14, 16, 55, 86–7, 121–2, 124–5, 142

Dagens Industri 20, 130
Dagens Nyheter 19–20, 127, 129
Distinguished Family Business Award 82–3
   criteria 1, 82
'do' phase 3, 39–42, 46, 51, 61, 67
Dumas, Jean-Louis 7, 8, 50, 57–8, 89, 91, 92
Dumas, Robert 8, 91

EID Parry 16, 115–16, 117
environment, respect for 14, 18, 106, 111, 124–5, 142
Expressen 129

family *see* four interest levels

Family Business Network (F.B.N.) 58
   Annual World Conference 81, 82
family businesses
   academic research 80–1
   entrepreneurial type 25–6
   ephemeral type 24
   importance of 81
   oldest surviving 80
   preserving type 24–5
   pruning 2, 25–6, 27, 65
   role of family 26–8
   and secrecy 81
   threats to multigenerational survival 23–33
family vision 3, 64–7, 79
Fellini, Federico 139
Forsell, Marcus 135
four interest levels 3, 28, 32–3, 34, 78
   and generational transition process 34, 38, 40–8

General Electric 32
generational transition process 28–33
   advice for incoming generation 36
   advice for outgoing generation 36–7
   challenges 31–3, 34–48
   communication between generations 35, 37, 40–1, 54–5
   as evolutionary process 38–45
   facilitating 36–7, 118–19
   and four interest levels 34, 38, 40–8
   and independent outside advice 61–4
   and intergenerational conflict 29–30, 31, 34, 35, 40–1, 62
   leadership cycle 3, 39, 67, 78
      see also 'do' phase; 'lead to do' phase; 'let do' phase
   leadership phases matrix 46–8
   and parent–child relationship 37–8, 40–1, 42, 45, 61, 66
   planning for 10, 18, 30, 34, 36, 46, 63, 124
   recognition of successors 23, 32, 71–2
   and risk of failure 30–1, 40, 46–7
   visioning process 64–7
   see also leadership development

genetically modified organisms (GMOs) 142
Göteborgsposten 127
Grace 22, 139
Great Depression 5, 6, 15, 114, 122
Gutkind & Company 134–5

Hansen, Dick 124
Henkel family
  Christoph 103
  Emmy 100
  Fritz (founder) 11, 99–100
  Fritz, Jr 100
  Hugo 11, 100
  Jost 11, 100
  Jürgen Manchot 100, 102
  Konrad 11–12, 69, 100–2, 103
  Willy Manchot 100
Henkel Group 11–13, 99–104
  acquisition 12, 101
  diversification 12, 72–4, 101
  family control 12–13, 69, 103–4
  financial problems 101
  governance structure 12, 101–2
  Information Circle 103
  internationalization 12, 72–4
  and leadership development 54, 62, 65
  leadership transition 61, 69, 100–1
  and non-family CEO 12, 69, 101–2
  pension fund 99
  role of family 102–3
  stock offering 12, 102
Hercules 114–15
Hermès 7–9, 89–92
  company culture 92
  diversification 7–8, 75–6, 89–90
  financial autonomy 92
  geographic expansion 7, 89
  leadership development 57–8
  leadership transition 90–1
  product development 8, 89, 90–1
  and quality products 7, 8, 90
  role of family 91–2
  stock offering 8, 91
Hermès family
  Emile-Charles 90
  Emile-Maurice 8, 90–1
  Jean-Louis Dumas 7, 8, 50, 57–8, 89, 91, 92
  Robert Dumas 8, 91
  Thierry 8, 90
Hoshi Hotel 80

IMC Global 115
IMD 1, 5, 80, 82
Immelt, Jeffery 32
India
  independence 114
  industrialization 15
  joining WTO 68, 117
individual
  growth of 50–60, 78
  see also four interest levels
Initial Public Offering (IPO) 12, 102
innovation, linked to tradition 7, 9, 49, 55, 75

Johnson Bank 125
Johnson family
  Curt 19, 125–6
  Fisk 19, 125, 126
  Helen 19, 125, 126
  Henrietta 122
  Herbert Fisk 17, 121–2
  Herbert Fisk, Jr (HF) 18, 62, 122–3, 124
  Sam (son of HF) 17, 18–19, 62, 75, 121, 122–5, 126
  Samuel Curtis (founder) 17, 121, 124
  Winnie 19, 125, 126
  see also Samuel C. Johnson Family Enterprises
Johnson Family Foundation 19, 126
Johnson Outdoors Inc. 19, 125, 126
Johnson Wax Company 18, 121, 122, 123
JohnsonDiversey 19, 126
Jones, Reginald 32

Kamps Group 22, 141
Kolb's learning model 53–9
  abstract conceptualization 53, 56
  active experimentation 53, 57, 58
  concrete experience 53
  reflective observation 53

Kongo Gumi 80
Kristiansen family
  Godtfred Kirk Christiansen 6, 85, 86
  Kjeld Kirk 6–7, 85, 86, 87
  Ole Kirk Christiansen 5, 84
  see also LEGO Group

'lead to do' phase 3, 39, 40, 42–4, 46, 51, 61, 67, 69
leadership
  institutional 45
  and long-term tenure 29–30
  organizational 44
  personal 42
  qualities needed for 52
  specialization 56, 107, 114
leadership development 2, 3
  growing the role in the business 60–71, 78
  and growth of individual 50–60, 78
  and learning process 52–9
  phased 39–48, 49, 78
  and visioning process 64–7
learning process 52–9
  education 36, 56, 58, 65, 107
  family business seminars 55–6, 103
  interaction with senior family 54–5, 56, 108
  and outside experience 56–8, 91, 96, 109, 116–17
  role of senior generation 59–60
  sabbaticals 58, 87, 124
  stages of evolution 59
  see also Kolb's learning model
LEGO Group 5–7, 84–8
  board of directors 86
  Compass Management (CM) 87
  conservative financial management 6, 84
  diversification 5–6, 84
  and globalization 6, 7, 86, 87
  as good corporate citizen 6, 55, 86–7
  and leadership development 58, 85, 87
  non-family CEO 86
  product development 6, 85
  see also Kristiansen family
LEGO System of Play 6, 85
'let do' phase 3, 39, 40, 44–5, 46, 61, 67, 69, 75

Lombard Odier Darier Hentsch 5, 80, 82

management 25, 28
  see also four interest levels
management consultants see outside advisors
Manchot, Jürgen 100, 102
Manchot, Willy 100
Marieberg 20, 76, 132–3
Misko 139
Mudaliar, Sir A. Rarnaswami 114
Murugappa Corporate Board (MCB) 118–19
Murugappa family
  Algy 117
  AMM 15, 16, 113–14, 116, 118
  Dewan Bahadur (founder) 15, 113–14
  Muru 16, 117, 118
  Murugappa 15, 113–14, 116
  Murugappan 117, 118
  Murugu 120
  Muthiah 116, 117
  MV 16, 116, 118
  Subbiah 117, 118
  Vellayan 15, 113, 116
Murugappa Group 15–17, 113–20
  acquisitions 16, 115
  diversification 15–16, 114
  governance structure 16–17, 56, 116, 118–19
  leadership development 58
  leadership transition 68, 113–14, 117–19
  and non-family CEO 119
  philanthropy 16, 115–16
  role of family 116–17, 119

Oasi Zegna 111
Olsson, Hasse 130
outside advisors 16, 61–4, 65, 67, 71, 76, 86, 117
ownership 13, 20, 21, 22, 25, 28, 38
  shareholder identity 26–8, 29
  shareholder proximity 26, 27–8, 29
  see also four interest levels

Panoramica Zegna 14, 106, 111
Parmalat 24

Parry Agro 115–16
Parrys Confectionary Ltd 116
Pavesi 139
Pellegrin, Jonathan 84
Persil 11–12, 99
Philips 115
Proctor & Gamble 12, 125, 133, 140
Puig family
  Antonio (founder) 9, 10, 93, 94
  Antonio, Jr 9–10, 94, 98
  Manuel 98
  Marc 98
  Mariano 9–10, 69, 94, 98
  Mariano, Jr 98
  see also Corporacion Puig

Raghavan, NS 119
Raid insecticide 18, 123

Samuel C. Johnson Family Enterprises 17–19, 121–6
  acquisitions 18, 124
  diversification 18, 75, 123–4, 125
  governance structure 19
  human resources policies 18
  leadership development 18, 58, 62, 67, 123
  philanthropy 55, 121–2, 124–5, 126
  product development 123
  Product Plus 18, 55, 122, 123
  see also Johnson family
SC Johnson 19, 126
Schmidheiny, Stephan 80
Second World War 15, 21, 114
Sihler, Professor 101
Spain, membership of CEE 97

TI Cycles 117
Toyota 57
Tube Investments of India (TII) 114, 115

Universal, UK 114

vision statements 65–6
visioning process 64–7
Vitale, Marco 108–9, 110

Wagen, Monica 98
Ward, John L. 113
Welch, Jack 32
'wise growth' strategy 3, 49–77, 78–9
  and four interest levels 50, 71
  growing as an individual 50–60, 78
  growing the business 71–7, 78
  growing the role in the business 60–71, 78
Woeste, Albrecht 103
World Trade Organization 68, 117

Young Presidents' Organization 58

Zegna Confection 14, 107
Zegna family
  Aldo 14, 107, 108–9, 110, 111–12
  Andrea 110
  Angelo (founder) 13, 105
  Angelo (son of Ermengildo) 14, 106–9, 108–9, 110
  Anna 110, 111
  Benedetta 110
  Ermengildo 13–14, 51–2, 56, 105–7, 108
  Gildo 14, 57, 62, 109, 110, 111
  Laura 111
  Mario 106
  Paolo 14, 62, 109, 111
Zegna Group 13–15, 105–12
  geographic expansion 14, 110
  leadership development 51–2, 62, 105–6, 107, 108, 109
  move into retailing 73, 77, 110
  and non-family CEO 110
  and quality products 110
  social entrepreneurship 14, 106, 111
  vertical integration 74–5